Mastering Google Drive and Docs (With Tips)

By Saqib Khan

Disclaimer

The information presented in this book is based on the author's personal opinion, knowledge and experience. In any case, the author will not be held liable for the use or misuse of the information contained herein.

Credits

Cover image designed by Atiq Qadri

Table of Contents

4

Introduction

Google Drive is an amazing cloud storage service that offers superb features apart from the cloud storage service. For example; apart from storage, sharing and syncing features, you also get a fully featured online Word processor (Document), Presentation, Spreadsheet, Form and Drawing web applications. But that's not all; you can also connect many different third-party apps to Google Drive.

In this book you'll not only learn how to use Google Drive's online web interface and Desktop sync client, but you'll also learn about some very useful apps and extensions that connects with Drive and lets you make it a powerhouse.

Here's what Google Drive can do for you:

- The most obvious use would be storing, sharing and syncing files across all your connected devices. You just need to save a file to Drive and the file magically appears on all other connected devices!
- With Drive, you can take advantage of free online office applications like Document, Presentation, Spreadsheet, Form and Drawing. All these apps are feature rich, and are sufficient for any personal or business user.
- You can easily create a survey using Forms and then send it to all whom you wish to know the opinion of. All the responses are then saved in a separate spreadsheet in a neat and clear structure.
- Drive lets you collaborate i.e. you can share the document with others and let them work on your file – all changes are reflected in real time. Best of all, using the sharing feature of Drive is a piece of cake.
- Google Drive lets you open mostly any document online. This is very useful when you don't have that particular program installed on your computer to open the file. For example, you might not have PDF reader installed, and in such a case, you

simply need to upload the PDF to Google Drive and then read it using the online interface. If the file is already in your Drive, then there's no additional step required.

- Google offers you 15GB of unified storage for free, which is shared between Drive, Gmail and Google+ photos. Additional storage space can be purchased at a cheap price – 100GB for $4.99 per month, which is a lot cheaper compared to other cloud storage services.

Google Drive can do wonders for any personal or business user if it's used the right way. Without any further talk, let's get started.

Chapter 1: Getting Started with Google Drive

To get started with Google Drive, all you need is a Google account. You can create one for free from https://accounts.google.com/SignUp

We'll be taking a closer look at this process in detail at later chapters.

Before we start, let's clear up some terminologies that I've used in this book:

Online interface: This refers to online interface of Google Drive accessible at https://drive.google.com/

Sync client, program or application: This refers to the Google Drive sync client (Desktop application) for Windows.

Difference between Google Drive and Google Docs: It won't be a surprise if some users get confused between Google Drive and Google Docs. Google Drive is referred to a cloud storage service that allows you to store your documents, photos, videos and any type of file at one place. From the same Google Drive's interface, you can also access Google Docs, where you can create, share and collaborate on documents, spreadsheets, presentations, forms, and drawing.

When Google Drive was launched, Google integrated the complete Google Docs functionality into Google Drive, and made it much more than a mere online office suite. With Google Drive, now we can store just any file to the cloud and do much more. Don't worry; you'll get to know everything about Docs and Drive in later chapters.

Connected devices: These are devices that are connected to the same Drive account. You can connect your desktop, laptop, tablet and smartphone to a single Drive account by using the same login credentials on every device that you own. All devices will remain synced, which means that if you upload a file to Drive from one device, then that file will be made available to other connected devices also.

System Requirements

Google Drive on the web supports two of the most recent versions of the following browsers:

- Chrome
- Firefox
- Safari
- Internet Explorer

Google says "Other browsers might work with Google Docs, Sheets, and Slides. However, we can't guarantee that features will work as expected."

No matter which browser you use, you should enable cookies and JavaScript on your web browser.

Desktop Client

For those who want to run the Google Drive sync client on their Mac and PC, here are the operating system requirements:

For Windows

- Windows Vista
- Windows XP
- Windows 7
- Windows 8

For Mac

- Mountain Lion (10.8)
- Lion (10.7)
- Snow Leopard (10.6)

Download Google Drive from: https://tools.google.com/dlpage/drive

Mobile app

Google Drive is also available for iOS and Android platforms.

For Android smartphones and tablets:

Google Drive Android app is compatible with Android 2.1 and above. You can get it by searching for it on the Play Store.

For iPhone and iPad:

Google Drive is also available for iPhone, iPad and iPod touch. The app is compatible with iOS 5.0 or above.

You can get it from Apple App Store.

Google Drive Storage Plans

Google gives you 15GB of free storage space which is shared between Drive, Gmail and Google+ Photos. With this combined storage space, you can use your storage the way you want. For example, you might be a heavy Gmail user but light on photos, which means you can use the free space anywhere – be it Gmail, Drive or photos.

The good part is that Google offers cheap storage plans compared to other cloud storage services like Dropbox. You can get 100GB storage space for $1.99 per month, 1TB for $9.99, and various other plans are also available.

Below is a table displaying Google's storage plans to be shared between Drive, Gmail and Google+ Photos.

Storage	Monthly Rate
100GB	$1.99
1TB	$9.99
10TB	$99.99
20TB	$199.99
30TB	$299.99

If we compare Drive's plan with Dropbox, then 100GB of Dropbox storage space costs $9.99 per month, whereas Drive offers the same 100GB plan for $1.99 per month. Drive is definitely super cheap compared to other cloud storage services.

To upgrade your storage plans, click on "Manage" from the bottom left of the Drive's online interface. Alternatively, you can head over to https://www.google.com/settings/storage/ and directly purchase new storage plans from there. However, for many of us, the shared 15GB storage space should be enough.

How to Sign Up for Google Drive

As you might have guessed, the first thing that you'll need to do is to sign-up for Google Drive but if you already have a Google account, then you can directly start using Google Drive. Just in case if you don't have a Google account, then simply follow the below steps to create one:

1. Go to drive.google.com and click on the red "Sign Up" button at the top-right corner of the screen.
2. You'll now be redirected to a page to create a new Google account. Enter all the details carefully on this page and click on "Next step."

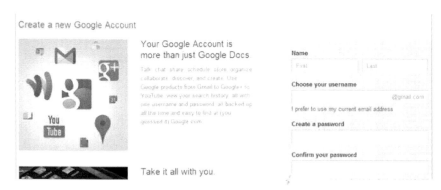

3. You can now add a profile photo from this page or click on "Next step."
4. That's it. You'll now get a message that says that you're ready to search, create and share across lots of Google products. Click on "Back to Google Docs" or you can simply visit drive.google.com to start using Google Drive.

You can also visit Google Drive by first going to www.google.com (signed-in), and then clicking on "Drive" from the top of the page.

Once you've created a Drive account, you can then login with the same details on Drive sync client that's installed on your computer or on the mobile app. In this book, we'll be taking a closer look at the web interface, and also at the sync program that's offered by Google Drive.

Chapter 2: Google Drive Web Interface Explained

In this chapter, we'll be taking a closer look at Google Drive's online web interface. You can access Google Drive from the web interface at drive.google.com. Once there, you can view the main interface of Google Drive – the central dashboard where everything happens.

On the left navigation bar, you'll be able to see the big red "Create" button and then the "Upload" button next to it. The Create button lets you create new document, presentation, spreadsheet, form, drawing or a folder. Also notice "Connect more apps" button that lets you connect more apps to your Google Drive account, but we'll be taking a look at it in a separate chapter. The "Upload" button, as the name suggests, allows you to upload any file to your Google Drive account.

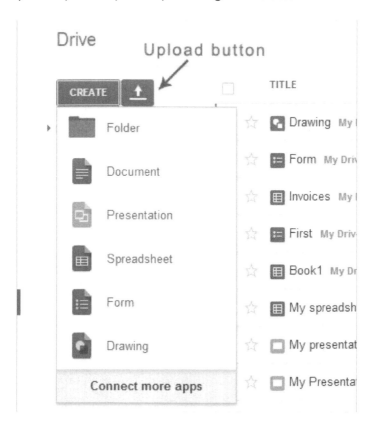

Below the Create button, you'll be able to see options for My Drive, Shared with me, Starred, Recent and More.

- My Drive: My Drive contains everything that you've ever created and uploaded to Google Drive so far.
- Shared with me: Files that others have shared with you.
- Starred: Files and folders that you've deemed as star-worthy.
- Recent: Everything you've recently viewed or worked on in the order it was last updated.

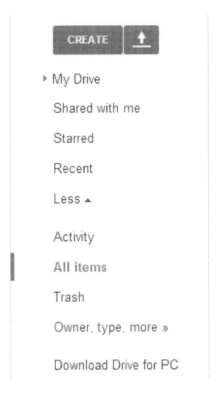

Click on "More" and you'll be presented with more options.

- Activity: Everything in your Google Drive in the order it was last updated.
- Offline: From here, you can enable offline editing. More details on this will be covered on a separate chapter.

- All items: Displays all items that you've uploaded to Google Drive. The only thing that it won't display is the Trash items.
- Trash: As the name suggests, it contains all the deleted files. Note that you can only trash items that you own. For items that you don't own, you can select Remove from the "More" menu.
- Owner, type and more: It basically opens advanced option that lets you search certain type of files in a breeze. You can apply filter based on type (all documents, images, PDF, tables, videos, spreadsheets and more), visibility (public, anyone with the link, private, not shared), Ownership (owned by me, not owned by me, opened by me, created with). Let's say you want to find all PDF files in your Google Drive. Simply open this advanced options and click on "PDF" to open search results containing only PDF files. You don't even need to enter the name of the file.

Let's delve deeper and learn about the action buttons, sorting, view and other buttons in detail. When you select a file, you'll be able to see action buttons that lets you perform actions for the selected file. In the below screenshot, buttons labeled from number 2-6 are action buttons.

1. New Folder: Creates a new folder in the current location.
2. Share: Click on this button to quickly share the selected file with others. You can then invite people to collaborate on your document.
3. Move to: You can move the selected file to other folder using this button.
4. Remove: Deletes the selected file or folder. Note that you won't get any notification asking you about this action and therefore

use this button only if you're sure that you want to delete that file or folder. The deleted file will be sent to the Trash folder from where you can delete it forever, or select it and restore it. After the file is deleted, you'll get a message that says "1 item was moved to the Trash" with a "Undo" link. If you want to restore the file, then click on Undo.

5. Preview: This button displays the preview of the file.
6. More: Clicking on "More" will open every possible option for the selected item. For example, you can preview, open, share, star, get details, move, rename, manage revisions, download, remove and perform many more actions from here.
7. Sort: Sort as last edited by me, last modified, last opened by me, title and by quote used.
8. List view: Switches to list view (this is the default setting of Google Drive).
9. Grid view: Switches to grid view.
10. Settings: Access advanced settings of Drive. You can change the display density, change upload settings, manage apps, know keyboard shortcuts, get help and open settings page.

You can view how much space you're utilizing in your Google Drive account from bottom left corner. There should be something written like 1% full.

Also notice stars next to item selection box. Stars allow you to mark important files for quick access. To "star" a file, simply click on the "star" icon and to remove it, click again. Alternatively, you can also do this by right-clicking on it to bring up the menu box and then clicking on "Add star."

Once starred, you can open all your starred items by clicking on "Starred" label from left side bar of Google Drive.

Lastly, you can use the search bar located next to the Google logo to search for particular files. Just try to remember the file name, enter it in the search box and hit enter. You can also click on the small down arrow to open advanced search options which allows you to search by type, visibility and ownership.

Creating a New Folder to Organize your Files

Folders help you to organize all your files, Google documents, spreadsheets, and presentations in Drive. Folders can also be shared with others. If you create a folder from the online interface, then the same folder is also created in your Google Drive sync program that you've installed on your computer.

Basically, if you make changes to a folder on the web, those changes will be reflected on your computer, and vice versa. And if you remove a file from the shared folder, collaborators with access to the folder will no longer see the item in their Google Drive.

How to create a new folder in Google Drive on the web:

1. Click on the red "Create" button at the top of left of your Google Drive.
2. Select "Folder" from the drop-down menu.
3. Enter a name of your new folder and then click on "Create". Alternatively, you can also click on the New Folder button from the toolbar directly to create a new folder at the current location.

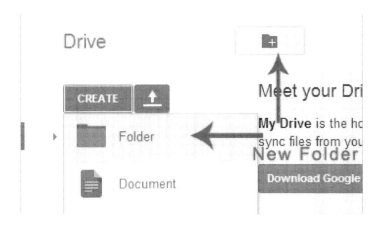

How to move a folder within another folder

To move a folder within another folder, you can simply drag and drop the folder into another. Alternatively, right-click the folder that you want to move and then select "Move to." Select the new folder where you want to move to, and click on "Move."

How to add a file to a particular folder

To add a file to a folder, simply drag and drop it to that particular folder. This method works great if you want to a few files to a folder, but if you want to move many files, then this method can be a real pain. That's why; let's take a look at the second method.

1. Select the item(s) by checking the box next to its title.
2. Click on the "Move to" icon (which would look like a folder icon).
3. Select the folder where you would like to move your items. You can also deselect a folder to remove a file from a particular folder.
4. Finally, click on "Move."

How to move a Google document, spreadsheet, or presentation to a folder

If you're working on a Google document, spreadsheet or presentation, then you can directly add that item to a folder without having to go back to your Drive. Here's how you can do it:

1. When the file is open, click on the Folder icon displayed to the right of the document's title.

2. Select the folder where you'd like to save your item. Or, you can also create a new folder from here.

Keyboard Shortcuts for Google Drive on the Web

If you're using Google Drive on the web, then you can use a variety of shortcut keys. These shortcut keys help you to accomplish different type of actions like selecting a document from a list, opening the document, creating a new document, and more. Here's a complete list of shortcut keys that you can try out when you're using the web interface of Google Drive.

Select items

Shortcut	Action
↓/j	Navigate to the next item in the list
↑/k	Navigate to the previous item in the list
x	Select/deselect the current item
Shift + ↓/j	Continue the selection/deselection to the next item
Shift + ↑/k	Continue the selection/deselection to the previous item
Shift + a	Select all visible items
Shift + n	Clear all selections

Go to different views

Shortcut	Action
g then n	Focus the navigation panel

g then f	Focus the folders view
g then l	Focus the items view
g then d	Focus the details pane
g then t	Focus the Google bar at the top of the page

Application

Shortcut	Action
?, Shift + /, or Ctrl + /	Display the keyboard shortcuts pop-up
d	Show/hide the details pane
/	Focus the search box

Create new Google documents, spreadsheets, and presentations

Shortcut	Action
Shift + t	Create a new document
Shift + p	Create a new presentation
Shift + s	Create a new spreadsheet
Shift + d	Create a new drawing

| Shift + f | Create a new folder |
| Shift + o | Create a new form |

Menus

Shortcut	Action
C	Open the create menu
U	Open the upload menu
A	Open the more actions menu
R	Open the sort menu
T	Open the settings menu

Actions

Shortcut	Action
Enter or o	Open the current item
n	Rename the current item
.	Share the selected items
z	Move the selected items

s	Star/unstar the current item or the selected items
p	Show document preview

Note that Mac users can replace Ctrl key with the Command key and Alt key with the Option key.

Chapter 3: Google Drive Sync Client for your Computer

Why should you install the sync client on your Computer?

Of course you can use only the online web interface of Google Drive and be happy, but then you wouldn't be taking full advantage of Google Drive. The web interface no doubt works great, but the Google Drive sync client for computer allows you to keep your local files synced with the files on the web. In a simple sense, Google Drive desktop app allows you to upload and sync files to Google Drive from your computer's desktop.

Let's say you've uploaded a new document, or a file using the web interface. If you've installed Google Drive client, then the next time your computer syncs, you'll have the same file on your computer too. This sync process is handled automatically which means you don't need to do anything manually. Vice versa, the moment you copy a file to your Google Drive folder on your computer, the same file will be automatically uploaded to the cloud, and thus, it will be available on all your connected devices and on the web too. Well, that's the beauty of cloud storage services like Google Drive, and you don't need to do anything manually.

How to Install Google Drive on your computer

To install the Google Drive application on your Windows computer, simply follow the below steps:

1. Head over to https://drive.google.com and click on "Download Drive for PC." The file will be downloaded to your computer.
2. Open the same file (googledrivesync.exe) to get started with the installation. You might receive a warning that Google Drive is an application downloaded from the Internet. Click on the "Open" button.
3. You'll now be able to see the below screen. Click on "Sign in now."

4. Next, enter your Google email and password in the window and click on "Sign in." Also make sure that "stay signed in" is selected.

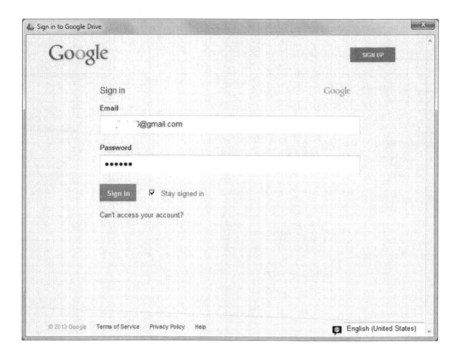

5. You'll be able to see getting started steps. The Google Drive client will inform you that a Google Drive folder will be created on your computer, and files in this folder will be available on all your devices. Click on "Next."

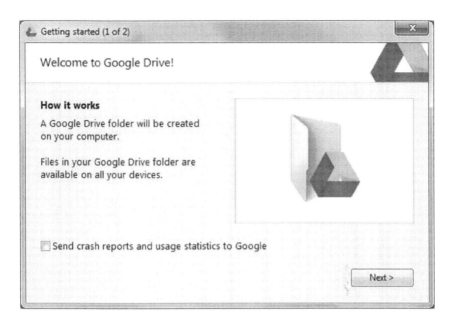

Welcome to Google Drive!

How it works

A Google Drive folder will be created on your computer.

Files in your Google Drive folder are available on all your devices.

☐ Send crash reports and usage statistics to Google

Next >

6. If you want to change the Google Drive folder location, then click on "Advanced setup" and then change the location. Else, click on the "Start sync" button to finish the process. With this step done, you have successfully installed Google Drive on your computer. Google Drive will now sync all files that you've stored in your account (if any), and if there are any files in your account, then you'll be able to see them on your local Google Drive folder on Desktop.

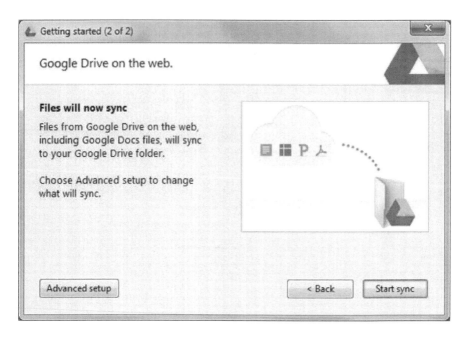

Now, there are three ways to open Google Drive folder on your computer.

1. Double-click the Google Drive folder on your Desktop.
2. In Windows Explorer, Google Drive folder will be added to your Favorites list.
3. You can also open the Google Drive folder on your computer by clicking on the Drive icon in your Windows taskbar and then selecting "Open Google Drive folder" from the menu.

You can now start adding files to this new Google Drive folder on your computer. Synced files will be displayed in "My Drive" section on the web.

Note that the uploading process can take some time depending on the file size. Once the file is uploaded, you will be able to see it on the web interface of Google Drive and on all other connected devices.

The Google Drive Folder will look like the below screenshot:

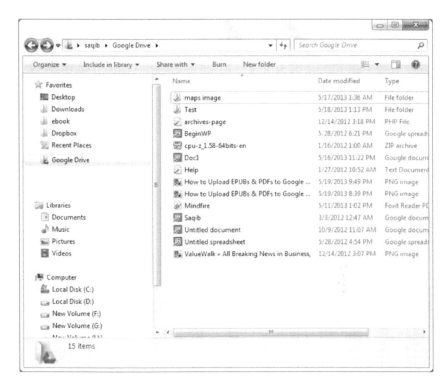

Notice the green tick mark with the files that are already uploaded online. For those files that are in the process of uploading, you'll be able to see a green sync icon. And once the file is uploaded, the icon will change to the tick mark.

Everything that you copy here either by drag and drop or by copy-paste, all those files will be uploaded to Drive and made available to all of your connected devices. Try placing one small file in this folder and then once uploaded, check it on the web interface at drive.google.com. Works magic, right!

When you right-click an item in your Google Drive folder, you'll see a menu that allows you to share that item and view it on the web.

Choose what syncs to your computer

The Google Drive application for your PC/Mac puts you in complete control – you choose what you want to sync or let the default settings work. You can choose exactly what you want to sync, be it your Google documents, presentations, spreadsheet, a particular folder in My Drive, or shared items.

To configure this setting, click on the Google Drive icon in the taskbar on your computer. Normally this would be upper right on Mac and lower right on PC.

Click on "Preferences" to open preferences window for Google Drive client.

In the sync options, check the box next to "Only sync some folders to this computer." Next, select the folders which you wish to sync and then click on Apply changes button. Note that after doing this, only your selected folders will be synced with the web, and nothing else.

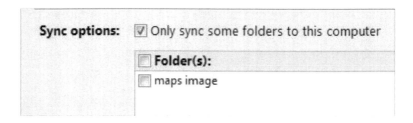

Note that by default, everything in My Drive will sync to your local Google Drive folder, unless you choose to sync individual folders.

All the shared files and folders won't sync to Google Drive folder on your computer, unless you add them to My Drive or to the individual folders. To do this, from the Preferences, click on "Visit shared with me to sync shared items." You'll be now taken to Google Drive on the web. From here, drag and drop shared files into My Drive or individual folders that you've created.

Configuring Google Drive on your Computer

Once Google Drive is installed, you'll be able to see it's icon on the system tray of your Windows computer. System tray is the area on taskbar located at bottom right of your screen, next to date and time. Click on the Drive icon to get more options from where you can configure Google Drive.

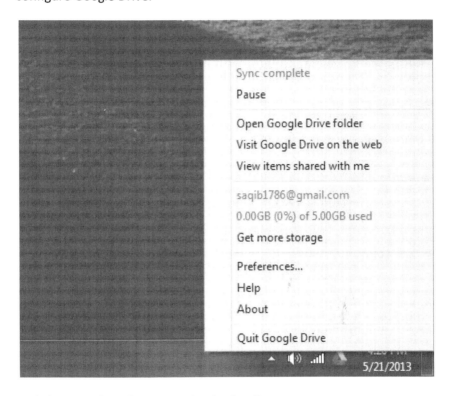

Let's learn each and every option in detail:

Pause: Pause the sync process for some time.

Open Google Drive folder: This will open Google Drive folder. Think of this as a shortcut to access your Drive folder. You can also open the same folder from the shortcut that's placed on your desktop.

Visit Google Drive on the web: Click on this option to visit Google Drive on the web using your default browser.

View items shared with me: Click on this option to view items that are shared with you.

Get more storage: If you're not satisfied by the free space offered, then you can purchase more space by clicking on this option.

Help: Stuck somewhere and need help? Visit Google Drive's support center on the web.

About: Displays the version number of Google Drive sync client installed on your computer.

Quit Google Drive: Quit/exit Google Drive from here.

Preferences: Opens the preferences window.

- Disconnect account: Disconnect your current Google account, and connect your Google Drive desktop folder to another Google Account.
- Get more storage: Purchase additional Google Drive storage
- Only sync some folders to this computer: Select which My Drive folders to sync to your computer. De-select the folders you don't want to sync.
- Sync Google Docs files: Check mark to sync all Google Docs files such as Document, Spreadsheet, Presentation and more.
- Start Google Drive automatically when you start your computer: Check mark to launch Google Drive automatically when you start the computer. The syncing process will also automatically start if this option is enabled.
- Send crash reports and usage statistics to Google: Share your feedback about how Google Drive performs on your PC or Mac. Disable it if you're concerned about your privacy.
- Show file sync status icons: Select to show file sync status icons.
- Proxy: Switch between "Direct connection" and "Automatically detect proxy" settings. For most of us, the default proxy settings work great.

After configuring preferences, don't forget to click on "Apply changes" button.

Chapter 4: Document

Google Documents (or Docs) is an online Word processing tool. Think of it as a Word processor like Microsoft Word, but with different set of features. You can create a new Document from the online web interface from drive.google.com. If you've enabled syncing Google Docs from your computers sync client's interface then the same file will appear in your computer also, but you won't be able to open it in any Word processor. That file will open directly in your default web browser.

The collaboration options of Documents make it a superb tool for anyone who's thinking to invite others to collaborate. You can share the document with others and all of them would be able to view and edit the document in real time.

Here's what you can do with Google Documents:

- Create and format text documents and collaborate with other people in real time.
- Upload a Word document and convert it to a Google Document.
- Adjust margins, space, font, color and more.
- Invite other people to collaborate on a document with you, giving them edit, comment or view access. You can choose what type of access you want to give to others.
- View your document's revision history and roll back to any previous version.
- Download a Google document to your desktop as a Word, OpenOffice, RTF, PDF, HTML or zip file.
- Translate a document to a different language.
- Email your documents to other people as attachments.

Now that you've got an idea on what Document is, let's move forward.

How to Create and Save a New Document

There are three different ways of getting started with Documents. You can create a new online document, you can upload an existing one, or you can use a template from templates gallery. First, let's learn how to create a new document.

To create a new document, go to drive.google.com and click on the red "Create" button and then select "Document" from the drop-down menu.

As soon as you name the document or start typing, Google Docs will automatically save your work every few seconds. Don't worry; you don't need to click on any Save button, as that task is handled automatically by Google Docs. At the top, beside the menu bar, you'll see text that indicates when your document was last saved. If you see a message that says "All changes saved in Drive," then it means that all of your current changes are saved to Drive.

Uploading a Document

You can upload your existing documents to Google documents at any time. When you're uploading, you can either keep your document in its original file type or convert it to Google Docs format. Converting your document to Google Docs format allows you to edit and collaborate online from any computer.

1. To upload a document, click on the "Upload" button (the red up arrow like button next to Create).
2. Click on Files.
3. Select the file and click on Open. The file will now start uploading and then you can see the upload process in a separate window.

.DOC and .DOCX formats can be easily converted to Google Docs format. After you've uploaded your document, you'll be able to see a small window at the bottom right corner. From the Settings of this window, click on "Convert uploaded documents to Google Docs format."

Creating a Document from a Template

Google Docs has some pre-built templates that you can start using right away. You can check out all templates from templates gallery section. Each template has standard text that you can replace with your own, and preset formatting that you can reuse. Templates thus, are very useful as they help you to start quickly, without the need to start from a scratch. For example; there are templates for recipe, resume, invoice, songwriting, etc.

You can also create a new document using Template by opening Documents and then navigating to: File -> New -> From Template.

Once there, click on "Use this template" button or if you want a preview, then click on the "Preview" button.

Editing and Formatting a Document

Now that you know how to create a new document, let's learn how to format the document. If you know how to use Microsoft Word, or OpenOffice, then you won't find it hard to use Google Documents.

Let's start with the toolbar. The buttons on the toolbar lets you do some basic things.

1. Print: Print the document.
2. Undo: Undo the last action.
3. Redo: Redo the last action.
4. Paint format tool: Google Docs lets you copy the formatting you've applied to a specific section of text to another section using the paint format tool. To use this tool, place the cursor where the text is formatted in the way that you want to copy. Then, click the paintbrush icon in your toolbar and select the text to which you want to apply the formatting to. The formatting from the original text will be copied to the selected text. Thus, you can quickly apply the same formatting to any text with this tool.
5. Change paragraph styles. Heading 1 is the biggest while Heading 6 is the smallest.
6. Font: Select the desired font from here.
7. Change font size: Change the font size from here.
8. Bold (Ctrl + B): Apply bold formatting to the text.
9. Italic (Ctrl + I): Apply italics formatting to the text.
10. Underline (Ctrl + U): Apply underline to the text.
11. Text color: Select a text color from here.
12. Text background color: Change text background color from here.

13. Insert a link: Select the text and then click on this button to insert a link. You can link the text to a website address, email address or a bookmark.
14. Insert comment: Insert a comment anywhere in the document. This is very useful if you want to add some important reminder or may be you want to inform something to the collaborators working on the same document.
15. Left align: Left align the text.
16. Center align: Center align the text.
17. Right align: Right align the text.
18. Justify: Justify the text.
19. Line spacing: Set line spacing from here.
20. Numbered list: Add numbered list to your document. For example; 1, 2, 3, 4, etc.
21. Bulleted list: Add bullet list to your document.
22. Decrease indent: Let's you decrease indent.
23. Increase indent: Let's you increase indent.
24. Clear formatting option: It removes any formatting that is applied to the text.

Tip: Simply hover your mouse over the button to know its function.

How to Insert Images, Link, Comment & More to Documents

You can insert many different elements to your document using the **Insert menu**. Click on Insert and then select what you want to insert to the document. You can insert image, link, equation, drawing, comment, footnote, special character, page number, bookmark and table of contents to the document.

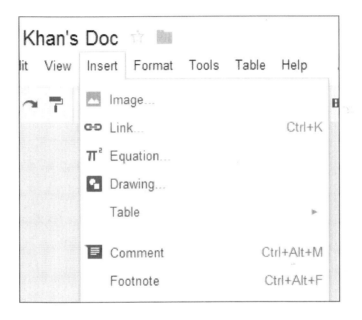

Inserting an Image

To insert an image to your document, click on Image from the Insert menu and then select the image from your computer or if you want to add the image from Google Drive, then click on "My Drive" and then select and insert the image. But that's not all – you can insert an image by taking a snapshot, from Picasa web album, from URL, or even search for images using Google Search.

Inserting a Link

You can insert a link to a website, an online document or to your email address. To do this, simply follow the below steps:

1. Select the text which you want to hyperlink.
2. Click on Insert -> Link.

3. If you want to link to a web address (website URL), then enter the full URL and click on OK. You can also change the "Text to display" field if you want to change the text of the hyperlink.
4. If you want to link to an email address, then select "Email address" and then enter the email.
5. If you've previously used Bookmark, then you can add that same bookmark from here. A bookmark is basically a link to a particular spot in your document. Let's say you want to send your document to a friend but that document is very long and he would find problem in locating the section that you want to highlight to him. In such a case, place your cursor where you want to add the bookmark and then go to Insert -> Bookmark. You'll see a blue ribbon added. Right-click and copy this link and then send it to your friend and he'll be able to open that exact same bookmark spot, and the document won't start from the

beginning as under normal circumstances. This is a very useful feature, especially for large documents.

Inserting a Comment

Comments are very useful feature of Google Documents. Comments help in adding notes to your regular document text and are visible to viewers as well as collaborators. It is invaluable for communicating with collaborators about specific parts of the document, as well as making notes about changes you've made or would like to make. When you publish your document as a webpage or print it, the comments will disappear.

To add a comment to your document, simply follow these instructions:

1. Place your cursor where you'd like your comment to appear or highlight text that you'd like to comment on.
2. Go to the Insert menu and select "Comment." For those who prefer keyboard - the shortcut key is Ctrl + Alt +M.

3. Type your comment in the box that appears to the right of the document, and click on the "Comment" button
4. To edit, delete or resolve the comment, click on the comment box and select the required option.

Same way, you can insert equation, drawing, footnote, special characters, horizontal line, page number, page count, page break, header, footer, bookmark and table of contents. We'll be taking a closer look at adding table of content in the next chapter.

How to Add Table of Content (Index) in a Document

Table of content is a very important part of document, especially if you're trying to stay organized. If you want to add table of contents in your document, then simply follow below steps.

1. Firstly, make sure that you've properly formatted the text. Chapter names should have Heading 1 style, and sub chapters should have Heading 2 style applied. You can select the style from the Styles icon on the toolbar as seen in the below screenshot.

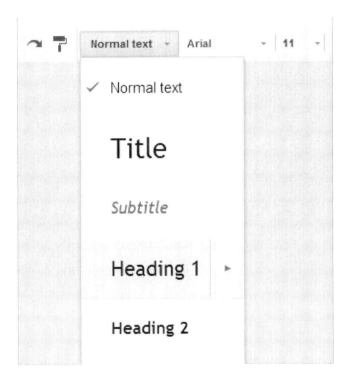

2. Once you've formatted the complete document as per the above instructions, it's time to add a table of content. Place your cursor where you want the table of content to appear and then go to Insert -> Table of Contents. Google Document will add a Table of Content with Heading 1 as the chapter names.

Best of all, those links are clickable, and clicking on it will take you to that chapters directly.

> # Table of Content
>
> Introduction
>
>   Getting started
>
> Why Us
>
> Services
>
> Contact us

If you update any headings, add, edit or remove any chapters, then click on this Table of Content and you'll be able to see a small "Update" button at the top right corner. Click on it to update your table.

Publishing, Printing & Downloading the Document to your Computer

Publishing a Document

Once you're done creating and editing your document, you can publish it as a webpage. To do this, go to File menu > Publish to the web. Next, click on "Start Publishing."

Publish to the web

Control publishing

☐ Require viewers to sign in with their Technostarry.com account
☑ Automatically republish when changes are made

Start publishing

Note: Publishing a doc does not affect its visibility option. Learn more

Close

Now you can copy the document link and then send it to your friends, co-workers and family. They can enter that link to the browser address bar to view the document. Of course, they won't be able to edit it or collaborate on this document.

Printing a Document

If you want a hard copy of the document then you can print it directly using Chrome, and if you're using some other browser like Firefox, Safari or Opera then you can download the file as PDF and then print it. For some reason, you won't be able to print directly if you're using any other browser except Chrome.

For Chrome users:

To print the document if you're using Chrome, go to File menu and then click "Print." A new dialog box will open where you can select your printer and do other settings. When you're ready, click on the Print button.

Google says that the document will print exactly as it appears in Google Docs, and that's why, there's no Print Preview option in Chrome.

For Firefox, Safari and other browser users:

To preview how your document looks before you print it, go to the File menu and click "Print preview." This will generate a preview of what your document will look like when it's printed on paper. To print the document, follow the below steps:

1. Go to File menu and click on "Print."
2. A PDF containing the document will automatically download. When the download completes, open the PDF.
3. In your PDF viewer, go to File menu and click on "Print."
4. Configure printing options and click on the Print button.

You can also download a document to another file format, and then print that file. To do this, go to File > Download as and then select the format in which you want to download the file. Once you've downloaded it, print the document.

Downloading a Document to your Computer

Google Docs work great online, but then you may want to download that document to your computer because Internet connection is not available at all places. Or you may just want to download the document for your record.

You can download the document as Microsoft Word (.DOCX), OpenDocument (.ODT), Rich Text format (.RTF), PDF document (.PDF), plain text (.TXT), and web page (HTML).

To download the document, go to File -> Download as and then select your preferred file format that you want to download the file in.

Once you do this, the download process will start automatically.

How to Add a Table in a Document

In Google Docs, you can also add a table, just like any other office suite. Presenting the data in a tabular form has its own advantages as not every kind of data can be presented in normal passages. Let's learn how to add a table in your Document.

Place the cursor where you want to add the table and then go to Table -> Insert table and then select the rows and columns that you want to add to the table.

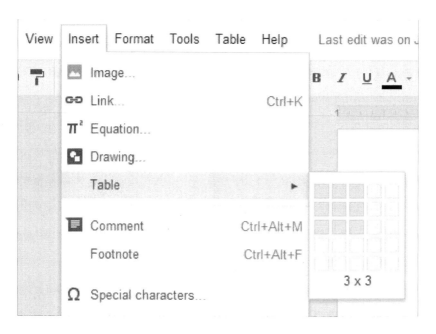

At maximum you can add 20 rows and 20 columns to the table. But after adding the table, if you want to add more rows, then place the cursor at the last cell of the last row and column (the bottom right cell), and then press the "Tab" key. This will add one more row to the table. Follow the same procedure to add more rows.

If you want to add more columns, then right click on any cell and select Insert column left or Insert column right. Same way, you can also find options for deleting rows, columns or entire table from this menu. If you want to add a border to the table, change cell background color and do more advanced settings then select Table properties and configure the settings.

How to Export (or Download) a Document

Once your Document is ready, you can download it to your Computer in various formats like Microsoft Word (.DOCX), OpenDocument format (.ODT), Rich Text Format (.RTF), PDF document (.PDF), Plain text (.TXT) and Web page (.HTML, zipped)

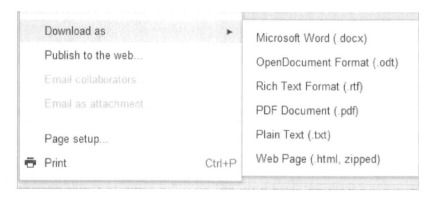

To download the document, go to File > Download as and then select the format that you want to download the file in. If you're going to run the presentation in Microsoft Word, then you should download the file in the same format.

Keyboard Shortcuts for Google Documents

Common actions	Shortcut
Select all	Ctrl + A
Copy	Ctrl + C
Cut	Ctrl + X
Paste	Ctrl + V
Undo	Ctrl + Z
Redo	Ctrl + Shift + Z
Compact controls	Ctrl + Shift + F
Print	Ctrl + P
Insert or edit link	Ctrl + K
Open link	Alt + Enter
Show common keyboard shortcuts	Ctrl + /
Save *Note: Every change you make is automatically saved in Drive*	Ctrl + S

Format text	Shortcut
Bold	Ctrl + B
Italicize	Ctrl + I
Underline	Ctrl + U
Strikethrough	Alt + Shift + 5
Superscript	Ctrl + .
Subscript	Ctrl + ,
Copy formatting	Ctrl + Alt + C
Paste formatting	Ctrl + Alt + V
Clear formatting	Ctrl + \

Edit and format paragraphs	Shortcut
Increase paragraph indentation	Tab
Decrease paragraph indentation	Shift + Tab
Apply normal text style	Ctrl + Alt + 0
Apply header style [1-6]	Ctrl + Alt + [1-6]
Left align	Ctrl + Shift + L

Center align	Ctrl + Shift + E
Right align	Ctrl + Shift + R
Full justify	Ctrl + Shift + J
Numbered list	Ctrl + Shift + 7
Bulleted list	Ctrl + Shift + 8
Move paragraph up/down	Alt + Shift + Up/Down arrow

Edit and access comments and footnotes	Shortcut
Insert comment	Ctrl + Alt + M
Open discussion thread	Ctrl + Alt + Shift + A
Enter current comment	holding Ctrl + Alt, press E then C
Move to next comment	holding Ctrl + Alt, press N then C
Move to previous comment	holding Ctrl + Alt, press P then C
Insert footnote	Ctrl + Alt + F

Enter current footnote	holding Ctrl + Alt, press E then F
Move to next footnote	holding Ctrl + Alt, press N then F
Move to previous footnote	holding Ctrl + Alt, press P then F

Application features	Shortcut
Find	Ctrl + F
Find again	Ctrl + G
Find previous	Ctrl + Shift + G
Find and replace...	Ctrl + H
Open revision history	Ctrl + Alt + Shift + G
Open research tool	Ctrl + Alt + Shift + I
Define selected word	Ctrl + Shift + Y
Word count	Ctrl + Shift + C
Toggle Input Controls	Ctrl + Shift + K

Open menus	Shortcut
Search the menus *(only in Compact controls)*	Alt + /
Context (right-click) menu	Ctrl + Shift + \
File menu	*in Google Chrome:* Alt + F *other browsers:* Alt + Shift + F
Edit menu	*in Google Chrome:* Alt + E *other browsers:* Alt + Shift + E
View menu	*in Google Chrome:* Alt + V *other browsers:* Alt + Shift + V
Insert menu	*in Google Chrome:* Alt + I *other browsers:* Alt + Shift + I
Format menu	*in Google Chrome:* Alt + O *other browsers:* Alt + Shift + O
Tools menu	*in Google Chrome:* Alt + T *other browsers:* Alt + Shift + T
Table menu	*in Google Chrome:* Alt + B *other browsers:* Alt + Shift + B

Help menu	*in Google Chrome:* Alt + H *other browsers:* Alt + Shift + H
Input Tools menu *(available in documents in non-Latin languages)*	Ctrl + Alt + Shift + K
Show your browser's context menu	Shift + right-click

Navigate around the document	Shortcut
Open header	holding Ctrl + Alt, press O then H
Open footer	holding Ctrl + Alt, press O then F
Move to next heading	holding Ctrl + Alt, press N then H
Move to previous heading	holding Ctrl + Alt, press P then H
Move to next heading [1-6]	holding Ctrl + Alt, press N then [1-6]
Move to previous heading [1-6]	holding Ctrl + Alt, press P then [1-6]
Move to next media *(image or drawing)*	holding Ctrl + Alt, press N then G
Move to previous media *(image or drawing)*	holding Ctrl + Alt, press P then G

Move to next list	holding Ctrl + Alt, press N then O
Move to previous list	holding Ctrl + Alt, press P then O
Move to next item in the current list	holding Ctrl + Alt, press N then I
Move to previous item in the current list	holding Ctrl + Alt, press P then I
Move to next link	holding Ctrl + Alt, press N then L
Move to previous link	holding Ctrl + Alt, press P then L
Move to next misspelling	Ctrl + ;
Move to previous misspelling	Ctrl + [

Navigate a table	Shortcut
Move to the start of the table	holding Ctrl + Alt + Shift, press T then S
Move to the end of the table	holding Ctrl + Alt + Shift, press T then D
Move to the next table	holding Ctrl + Alt + Shift, press N then T
Move to the previous table	holding Ctrl + Alt + Shift, press P then T

Move to the start of the table column	holding Ctrl + Alt + Shift, press T then I
Move to the end of the table column	holding Ctrl + Alt + Shift, press T then K
Move to the next table column	holding Ctrl + Alt + Shift, press T then B
Move to the previous table column	holding Ctrl + Alt + Shift, press T then V
Move to the start of the table row	holding Ctrl + Alt + Shift, press T then J
Move to the end of the table row	holding Ctrl + Alt + Shift, press T then L
Move to the next table row	holding Ctrl + Alt + Shift, press T then M
Move to the previous table row	holding Ctrl + Alt + Shift, press T then G
Exit Table	holding Ctrl + Alt + Shift, press T then E

Focus	Shortcut
Return focus to document text	Esc
Move focus to popup	holding Ctrl + Alt, press E then P

(for links, bookmarks, and images)	
Move to top of application	Ctrl + Alt + Shift + M
Chat	Shift + Esc
Focus containing webpage *(such as when using Docs in Google+ Hangouts)*	Ctrl + Shift + Esc

Use a screen reader	Shortcut
Enable screen reader support	Alt + Shift + ~
Speak selection	Ctrl + Alt + X
Announce cursor location	holding Ctrl + Alt, press A then L
Announce styles at cursor location	holding Ctrl + Alt, press A then S
Speak the table column and row header	holding Ctrl + Alt + Shift, press T then H
Speak the table cell location	holding Ctrl + Alt + Shift, press T then N
Speak the table row header	holding Ctrl + Alt + Shift, press T then R
Speak the table column header	holding Ctrl + Alt + Shift, press T

then C

Chapter 5: Presentation

Google slides have now been renamed to Presentation. It basically lets you to create Presentations (much like Microsoft Office's Powerpoint) with different slides in it. Any presentation that you upload to Drive will be converted to the latest version of Presentation.

Here are some of the features of Presentation:

- Simple and easy-to-use UI with no complicated options.
- See updates in real time as you collaborate with other people.
- Draw organizational charts, flowcharts, design diagrams and much more right within Presentation.
- Easily change background, theme, layout and transition from icons on the toolbar.
- Turn shapes within your presentation into hyperlinks to other slides, presentations, or external webpages.
- Collaborate with other people by adding comments to shapes, text or slides. Commenting is very useful especially when collaborating with others.

If you want to impress your friends or co-workers, then Presentation is surely a superb choice. Let's delve deeper and find out how it works.

How to Create, Insert, Duplicate and Delete Slides

To get started with Presentations, go to drive.google.com, click on the red "Create" button and then on "Presentation."

Next, you'll need to choose a theme that suits your needs. Select a theme and then click on OK. If you don't want to choose a theme every time it starts, remove the check from "Show for new Presentations." You can also click on the 'x' button at the top right to proceed without selecting any theme.

How to insert a new slide

There are four ways to insert a new slide into your presentation:

1. Click on the red + button from the toolbar.
2. Press Ctrl + M on Windows or CMD + M on a Mac for inserting a new slide.
3. Right click in the slide filmstrip and select New slide.
4. Go to Slide menu and then select New slide.

Same way, you can add as many slides as you want into your presentation. By default, the new slide will have a 'Title and Body' layout. To change this layout or apply a theme, go to the Slide menu, and select 'Change Layout' or 'Change Theme.' You can also click on the small down arrow next to the red + button to add a slide with a different layout.

How to duplicate a slide

To duplicate an existing slide, you can follow any ONE of the following methods:

1. Select the slide that you want to duplicate, go to Slide menu and then click on "Duplicate slide."
2. From the list of slides on the left, right-click the slide you want to duplicate, and select 'Duplicate slide.'
3. To duplicate multiple slides, hold the Shift key and select the slides you'd like to duplicate. Then, right click the selection and select 'Duplicate slide.'

How to delete a slide

To delete a slide, follow any ONE of the below methods:

1. From the list of slides on the left, right click on the slide that you'd like to delete and select Delete slide.
2. From the list of slides on the left, select the slide that you'd like to delete and press Delete from your keyboard.
3. Select the slide that you want to delete, go to the Slide menu and then click on Delete slide.

How to re-arrange or organize slides

You can reorder slides after you've created them. To reorder slides, you can simply drag and drop them to a new position from the list of slides on the left.

Press the Shift key to select a sequence of slides, or use the Ctrl key to select multiple, non-sequential slides. Now you can drag and drop the slides to a new position, or you can also go the Slide menu and select one option from:

- Move slide up.
- Move slide down.
- Move slide to beginning.
- Move slide to end.

The order of slide will change according to your selection.

How to Import a PowerPoint File

At times, you might be working with Microsoft PowerPoint or any other presentation application but then later on you decide to give Google Presentation a try. So here's how to import a file to Google Presentation.

Click on the red up arrow (upload) button in Google Drive to upload the file. In the bottom right corner, from Settings, make sure that "Convert uploaded file to Google Docs format" is selected.

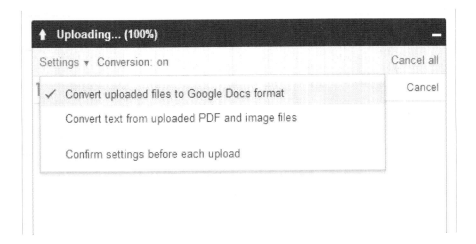

Once uploaded, you can now open the file by clicking on it from the web interface and it will open in Google Presentations. The best part is that Drive retains the same images, format, and animations when importing which means you don't need to apply the same formatting again.

You can also invite other people to work on the same file, which was not possible before when your file was just lying on your hard disk.

How to import a slide from another presentation

Importing slides is an easy way to reuse slides from an existing presentation. Instead of creating a new slide and working on its each element, you can import a slide from your other presentations and use it.

To import slides, follow below steps:

1. Go to the File menu and select "Import slides".
2. Next, select a presentation that's already saved in Drive or choose a presentation to upload from your computer by clicking on "Upload" and then on "Select a file from your computer". After selecting a presentation file, you can then select the slide(s) that you want to import.
3. Use the "Select Slides: All" option to quickly select all slides, or manually select slides that you'd like to import.
4. Leave the box next to "Keep original theme" checked if you'd like to import your slides unmodified. Uncheck the box if you'd like the slides to fit into the look of your new presentation.
5. Click "Import Slides" to finish.

If you receive an error during the importing process, then it might be because it is larger than 50MB, or because the file is not supported by Google Presentations. The file should only be in .PPT or .PPTX format, as well as any Google Presentation.

How to Insert Image, Video, Text Box, Word Art, Shapes & Table to a Presentation

Inserting an image, video, text box, word art, shapes and table to a presentation is very easy, in fact, it's a piece of cake. Go to the Insert menu and click on the respective button to insert the element of your choice.

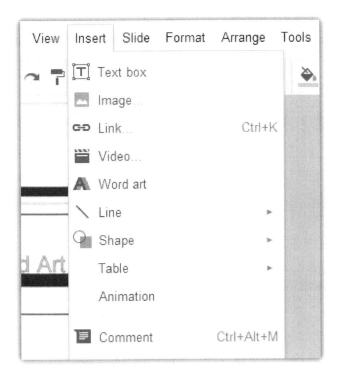

For example; click on Word Art to insert Word Art and then enter the text. Next, hit enter to save changes and insert the Word Art.

Same way, you can insert many other elements like images, videos, shapes, tables, comment and more using the Insert menu.

Tip: Once you've inserted a shape for example, right-click on it to change its order (bring to front or back) or to rotate it.

How to Change or Add a Theme to the Slide

To change or add a theme to your presentation, go to the Slide menu, and select Change theme. Alternatively, you can also directly click on the Theme button from the toolbar.

Select the theme that you'd like to use and click on OK.

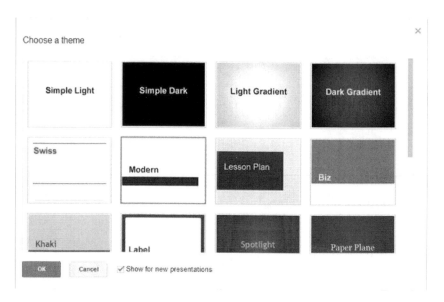

Note that the theme will be applied to all the slides in the presentation and not just to a single slide.

How to Change or Add a Background Image to the Slide

You can change the background color as well as set a custom image for each of your slide. You can change these settings for a single slide or for all of the slides in your presentation.

To do this, simply click on the "Background" button from the toolbar. Alternatively, you can also go to the Slide menu and click on "Change background."

From here, you can change the background color, choose a custom image for your slide or reset the background to the theme's background. Once you make these changes, click on "Done" to apply the settings to only the selected slide, or click on "Apply to all" to apply the same settings to all the slides.

How to Change the Layout of the Slide

To change the layout of the slide, select a slide and then click on the "Layout" button from the toolbar. Alternatively, you can also go to Slide > Change layout.

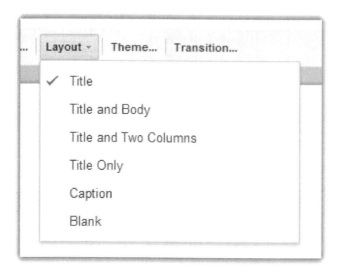

Next, select the layout that suits your presentation and it will be applied instantly.

How to Add Animations to a Slide

Animations make your presentation stand out. It makes your slide looks more dynamic, and they're also a great way to reveal text or objects on a slide one step at a time. For example, you could set up animation such that you can reveal five bullet points of text one-by-one with each click. Presentations allow you to apply many different types of animations.

To add animations to the slide, you'll need to open the Animation pane. To do this, follow any ONE of the following three methods:

- Go to the View menu and click on Animations. The Animations pane will appear on the screen in the right side.
- Select a slide and then click on the Transitions button from the toolbar.
- Right-click on any object and then click on Animate.

Now that the animations pane is visible, you can start applying the animation effect that you like. First, you'll need to apply an effect such as Fade, flip, slide from right, slide from left, cube or gallery. Let's say you would like to apply the Fade effect. Click on "Fade" and then adjust its speed by selecting it from Slow, Medium or Fast. Next, click on Fade in and then select the type of fade effect you would like to apply. Click the "On click" menu to set the timing for the shape's animation. Once you've applied the animation, click on the Play button to see a preview. You can also go to View > Present (Ctrl + F being the shortcut key) to view a full screen preview.

You can add as many animations to a slide as you'd like, with one animation per shape. To add an animation to a shape, click **+Add animation** in the Animations pane and then the object to which the effect will be applied will be highlighted. You can also select a different object from here to apply the animation to that object. Alternatively, you can also select a shape and then right-click on it and click on Animate.

Note that the list of animations pane is displayed in the order in which animations will take place on the slide. Once an animation is listed in the Animations pane, you can drag an animation up or down to change the order in which shapes appear or disappear on the screen. To delete animations from a shape, click Delete (small x) next to that animation entry.

Overall it can be said that animations are a way to add some fun to the boring slide.

Note: Cube, Gallery and Flip transitions do not work when viewing a presentation in Internet Explorer 9.

How to Export (or Download) a Presentation

Once your Presentation is ready, you can download it to your Computer in various formats like Microsoft PowerPoint (.PPTX), PDF document (.PDF), Scalable Vector Graphics (.SVG), PNG image (.PNG), JPEG image (.JPG) and plain text (.TXT).

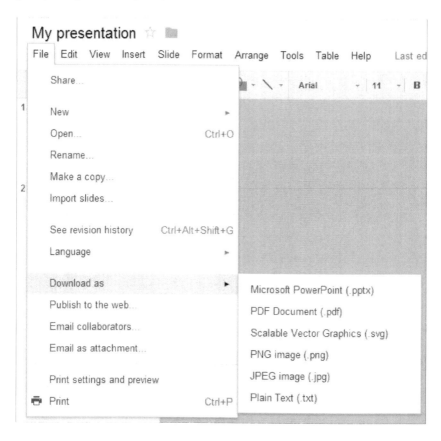

To download the presentation, go to File > Download as and then select the format that you're comfortable with. If you're going to run the presentation in Microsoft PowerPoint, then you should download the file in the same format. The PPTX format is also compatible in OpenOffice and some other office suites.

How to Apply Slide Transitions

Slide transitions are those effects that are applied when you move from one slide to another. Applying these transition effects is very easy.

You can add or modify slide transitions from the Animations pane. To open this Animations pane:

Click on the Transition button from the toolbar or go to the Slide menu and click on "Change transition."

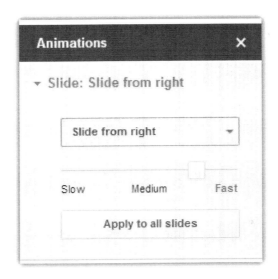

The Animations pane is split into two levels. At the top, you'll see transition options. Use the drop-down menu to select a slide transition for the selected slide. Next, select a transition speed by moving the bar. If you want to apply the same transition to all slides, then click on "Apply to all slides." Once you're done applying transition effect, click on the Play button to see a preview.

How to Publish Slide (or Presentation) on the Web

Publishing allows you to make your Google Presentation available on the web. Once you publish a Presentation, you get a URL that you can share with anyone.

To publish, simply follow the below steps:

1. Go to the File menu and click on Publish to the web
2. Click on "Start Publishing" button. You'll now get a notification asking you if you really want to publish this document. Click on OK.
3. You will now get a link to the published document. You can share this link to anyone that you'd like to access your item.

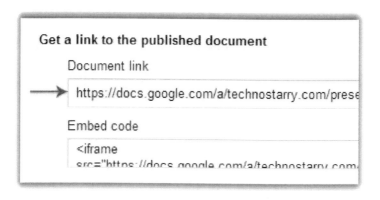

Your file will be accessible from this URL until you either delete your file or choose to stop publishing. To stop publishing, open the publishing dialog again and click the "Stop publishing" button. If you do this, anyone clicking the link to the published item will no longer be able to access it.

Keyboard Shortcuts for Google Presentations

Keyboard shortcuts can help you save a lot of time if you're faster on keyboard than your mouse. Here's a complete list of actions you can do in Google presentations using your keyboard.

Navigation

Shortcut	Action
Ctrl + Alt + B	Open animations panel
Ctrl + Alt + G	Open revision history panel
Ctrl + Alt + S	Open speaker notes panel
Ctrl + Alt + F	Move to filmstrip
Ctrl + Alt + C	Move to canvas
Page Down	Move to next slide
Page Up	Move to previous slide
Tab	Select next shape
Shift + Tab	Select previous shape
Home	Go to first slide
End	Go to last slide
Ctrl + Shift + Right	Zoom in
Ctrl + Shift + Left	Zoom out

Objects

Shortcut	Action
Ctrl + D	Duplicate shape
Ctrl + G	Group selection
Ctrl + Shift + G	Ungroup selection
Ctrl + Up	Move forward
Ctrl + Down	Send backward
Ctrl + Shift + Up	Bring to front
Ctrl + Shift + Down	Send to back
Shift + Move	Move vertically or horizontally
Shift + Rotate	Rotate in 15° rotation increments
Shift + Resize	Resize, keeping object's aspect ratio

Shift + Up, Down, Left or Right	Nudge one pixel at a time

Slides

Shortcut	Action
Ctrl + M	Insert slide
Ctrl + Down	Move slide down in filmstrip
Ctrl + Up	Move slide up in filmstrip
Ctrl + Shift + Up	Move slide to beginning
Ctrl + Shift + Down	Move slide to end

Selection

Shortcut	Action
Ctrl + Alt + X	Read current selection
Shift + mouse selection	Add to selection
Alt + mouse selection	Add only completely enclosed shapes to selection

Comments

Shortcut	Action
Ctrl + Alt + M	Insert comment
Shift + Esc	Open chat sidebar
J	When focus is on comment, move to next comment
K	When focus is on comment, move to previous comment
R	When focus is on comment, reply to comment
E	When focus is on comment, resolve comment

Spelling

Shortcut	Action
Ctrl + ;	Move to next spelling correction
Ctrl + [	Move to previous spelling correction

Menu navigation

Shortcut	Action
Ctrl + Alt + F	Open File menu
Ctrl + Alt + E	Open Edit menu
Ctrl + Alt + V	Open View menu
Ctrl + Alt + S	Open Slide menu
Ctrl + Alt + O	Open Format menu
Ctrl + Alt + B	Open Table menu
Ctrl + Alt + H	Open Help menu

Text formatting

Shortcut	Action
Ctrl + B	Bold
Ctrl + I	Italics
Ctrl + U	Underline
Ctrl + . (period)	Superscript
Ctrl + , (comma)	Subscript
Ctrl + / (forward slash)	Clear formatting

Paragraph formatting

Shortcut	Action
Ctrl + Shift + L	Align left
Ctrl + Shift + J	Justify
Ctrl + Shift + R	Align right
Ctrl + Shift + 7	Numbered list
Ctrl + Shift + 8	Bullet

Chapter 6: Spreadsheet

Google Spreadsheet is an online application that lets you create spreadsheets and simultaneously work with other people. Spreadsheet can be compared with Microsoft Excel and other such applications but it does not offer all of Excel's advanced features.

Some might think that spreadsheets can only be used by people to process complicated numbers and data, but in reality it can actually be used for a variety of everyday tasks. Spreadsheet can help you in financial matters, planning a budget, creating an invoice, number crunching tasks and many other such day to day tasks.

Here are some of the tasks that you can perform in Google Spreadshseet:

- Import and convert Excel, .csv, .txt and .ods formatted data to a Google spreadsheet
- Export Excel, .csv, .txt and .ods formatted data, as well as PDF and HTML files
- Chat in real time with others who are editing your spreadsheet
- Use formula editing to perform calculations on your data, and use formatting make it look the way you'd like
- Create charts/graphs with your data
- Embed a spreadsheet or individual sheets of your spreadsheet on your blog or website

How to Create a New Google Spreadsheet

There are three different ways of getting started with Google Spreadsheets. You can create a new Google spreadsheet, you can upload a spreadsheet from a computer, or you can use a template from templates gallery.

To create a new spreadsheet, go to your Google Drive's web interface at drive.google.com click on the red "Create" button and then select Spreadsheet from the drop-down menu.

Next, you can give a name to your spreadsheet by clicking on "Untitled spreadsheet" above the menu bar, and then entering a new name for your file. As soon as you start typing, Drive will automatically save your work every few seconds which means you don't need to click on any save button manually.

At the top of the document, you'll see text that indicates when your document was last saved. If the most recent changes are saved, then you'll see a message that says "All changes saved in Drive." You can access all your documents at any time by logging-in to your Google Drive account.

How to Upload an Existing Spreadsheet to Google Docs

When you're uploading a spreadsheet, you can either keep your spreadsheet in its original file type or convert it to Google Docs format. Converting your spreadsheet to Google Docs format will allow you to edit and collaborate online.

You can upload the following file types:

- .xls and .xlsx
- .ods
- .csv
- .tsv
- .txt

- .tsb

Follow these steps to upload a spreadsheet:

1. In your Google Drive's web interface, click on the red "Upload" icon.
2. Click "Files" and then select the document that you'd like to upload.
3. You'll now see an Uploading screen on the bottom right. From Settings, make sure that "Convert uploaded files to Google Docs format" is selected. You need to do this setting only if you want to edit and collaborate on the document online, else there's no need for this.

Note that uploaded files that are converted to Google spreadsheets format can't be larger than 20 MB and should be under 400,000 cells and 256 columns per sheet.

How to Create a Spreadsheet from a Ready Made Template

For those who don't want to start from scratch, they can quickly create a spreadsheet by picking one of the ready-made templates.

Each template has standard text that you can replace with your own, and preset formatting that you can reuse. Just click on it and replace the text with your own.

After visiting the templates gallery, you can click on the Preview button to see a preview, or click on the "Use this template" button to use it.

Editing and Formatting a Spreadsheet

If you've used any other spreadsheet application (like Microsoft Excel), then you're already familiar with how this works. To enter content in an empty cell, click on the cell and start typing. To move between cells, use the arrow keys. To edit a cell that already has content, double-click the cell and edit the content. Alternatively, you can click the cell once and press Enter or F2 to edit it.

If you want to create line breaks within a cell, then place your cursor in a cell and then press Ctrl+Enter.

Formatting a Spreadsheet

You can format data in your spreadsheets in a variety of ways using the options present in the toolbar. You can hover over an icon on the toolbar to see a message describing what that option can do.

These formatting options are available in the toolbar:

- Print: As you might have guessed, this option allows you to print the spreadsheet.
- Undo: Undo the last action.
- Redo: Redo the last action.
- Paint format: Apply the same formatting to some other content.
- Format as currency: Select the text that you want to format as currency and then click on this option.
- Format as percent: Select the text that you want to format as percent and then click on it.
- More formats: Click on it to select more formatting options.
- Font: Select the font from here.

- Font size: Change the font size from here.
- Bold: Apply bold formatting to the text.
- Italic: Apply italics formatting to the text.
- Strikethrough: Apply a strikethrough to the selected text (~~like this~~).
- Text color: Select a text color from here.
- Fill color: Fill a color to the entire cell.
- Border: Apply a border to the cell. You can also select a number of cells and then apply borders to all of them at once.
- Merge cells: Merge multiple cells to one.
- Horizontal align: Helps you to align the text horizontally.
- Vertical align: Helps you to align the text in vertical position.
- Wrap text: Click to wrap text.
- Insert comment: Insert a comment anywhere in the sheet. This is very useful if you want to remember an important point, or may be you just want to inform something to the collaborators that are working on the same file.
- Insert chart: Inserts a chart.
- Filter: Select the data that you want to filter and then click on it.
- Functions: Add mathematical functions to your spreadsheet with this option.

To perform these functions, simply select the range of cells and then click on the respective button from the toolbar. Alternatively, you can use keyboard shortcuts which you'll be learning at later chapters.

You can add a new sheet to the current spreadsheet by clicking on the + icon at the bottom left of the screen as shown in the below screenshot. You can add multiple sheets to a single file, just like you do in a spreadsheet program on your computer.

35				
36				
37				

+   ≡ | Sheet1 ▾ | Sheet2 ▾ | Sheet3 ▾

From here, you can also switch between different sheets by clicking on the name of the sheet. Right-click on a sheet's name and you'll get options like Delete, Duplicate, Copy to, Rename, Protect sheet, Hide sheet and Move right/left.

The "Protect sheet" option allows you to select who can edit the sheet. It basically lets you protect your sheet from being edited by collaborators. If you want that only you should be able to edit the sheet, then select "Only me", if you want anyone who's a collaborator to edit the sheet then click on "Anyone invited as collaborator" and if you want to select some specific collaborators then click on "Me, and the collaborators listed below."

How to Format Numbers, Date, Time, Currency & More

You can format numbers in a spreadsheet in a variety of ways, such as percent, decimal and scientific notation. You can also ensure that your date, time and currency are properly displayed in the spreadsheet.

To apply such formatting to numbers, dates, currencies and more, follow below steps:

1. Select the range of cells you'd like to format.
2. Click on "123" icon from the toolbar.
3. Select what type of formatting you want to apply to the selected range.

Tip: You can also use the Paint Format tool to apply the same formatting to a different text.

How to Add Formulas to a Spreadsheet

As you might have guessed, spreadsheet can perform mostly any number crunching task, but to do this, you'll need to use formulas (or functions) which are really easy to use.

You can add a formula to any cell in a spreadsheet by typing an equal sign (=) followed by the name of the function. Spreadsheet will show a box displaying the name and syntax of the formula that you're building.

Let's learn how to perform a simple sum function in spreadsheet.

Adding up rows or columns of numbers is one of the most common operations carried out in a spreadsheet. Every function has some syntax which you need to follow, in order to apply that function properly. Syntax can include the function's name, brackets and arguments. The syntax for the SUM function is:

=SUM(number_1,number_2,....number_30)

This means that up to 30 numbers can be summed by this function.

So let's say you want to perform the SUM for cells A1 to A5. To do this, follow below instructions:

1. Place your cursor where you want the result to appear. For example; in cell A6.
2. Type =SUM(A1:A5) and press Enter. As you can see in the formula, we simply followed the above syntax. A1:A5 (read it as A1 to A5) means the range of cells of which we need the sum of. You can now see the result in the cell. The formula which was applied in the cell can be viewed from the functions bar, or by double clicking on the cell.

3. There's also another way where you don't need to remember this syntax. After placing your cursor where you want the result to appear, go to Insert > Function > Sum. Next, select the range for which you want to perform the sum and then press Enter.

Google Spreadsheets supports many cell formulas which are typically found in most desktop spreadsheet applications. These formulas can be used to create functions that manipulate data and calculate strings and numbers. To view a complete list of all these formulas, go here http://bit.ly/functionlist.

When using these formulas, don't forget to add quotation marks around all function components made of alphabetic characters that aren't referring to cells or columns.

Some More Formula Examples

All formulas should always begin with an equal (=) sign. The standard mathematical operators can be used in the formulas. For example:

Addition	+(plus sign)
Subtraction	-(minus sign)

Multiplication	*(asterisk)
Division	/(forward slash)
Exponents	^(caret)

By combining a mathematical operator (like above) with cell references, you can create a variety of simple formulas in Google Spreadsheets. Formulas can also include a combination of a cell reference and a number.

Let's take a look at some simple formula examples that you can use in spreadsheets.

Formula	What it does
=SUM(A1:A10)	Adds cell content from cell A1 to A10
=A1+A2+A3	Adds cell A1, A2 and A3
=A5*A10	Multiplies cell A5 to cell A10
=A5*10	Multiplies cell A5 by 10

How to Create a Series of Numbers in Spreadsheet

What's a series of numbers? Let's say you want to write a series from 10 to 50. Would you manually type all this? There's no need to write it manually, as there's a smarter way to do this in spreadsheet.

To create a series of numbers in the spreadsheet, follow these instructions:

1. Type the first number of the series into a cell. Below that cell, type the second number of the series. Let's say you've entered 50 in cell A10 and 51 in cell A11.
2. Select both the cells and click the small blue square in the lower-right corner of the cell. Drag the mouse down until you reach the cell where you want to stop. A series of numbers will now be created in the selected cells.

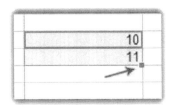

This way, you can quickly create a series of numbers, without typing everything manually, and thereby saving time.

If Auto-Fill recognizes a pattern in the content of the selected cells, it fills in the remaining items to complete the pattern. If Auto-Fill doesn't recognize a pattern, it will just repeat the content that was highlighted.

How to Import a Spreadsheet

You can import a spreadsheet in many different formats such as:

- .xls
- .xlsx
- .ods
- .csv
- .txt
- .tsv
- .tsb

However, note that password protected files cannot be imported. To import a spreadsheet, go to File > Import.

Next, choose the file to upload and then select your preferred import action.

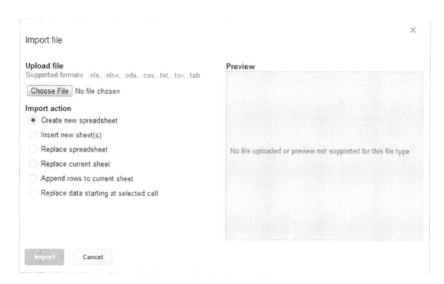

Here's detailed information on each option:

- **Create new spreadsheet**: This option creates a new Google spreadsheet from your imported file in a new browser tab.

- **Insert new sheet**: This option adds new sheets to your existing spreadsheet containing the data in your imported file.
- **Replace spreadsheet**: This option replaces your existing spreadsheet with the data in your imported file.
- **Replace current sheet**: This option replaces the current sheet with the imported data. Formatting and data previously on this sheet is replaced.
- **Append rows to current sheet**: This option adds the imported data to the row after the last row with any data in it on your current sheet. Your existing data will remain intact.
- **Replace data starting at selected cell**: This option pastes the imported data in a range of cells you have selected. It will replace any data that was previously on the sheet where the imported data has been pasted, but preserves existing data everywhere else.

Note that not all file types will have all six options.

How to Merge Cells in a Spreadsheet

Merging two or more cells is very easy. To merge cells horizontally or vertically in a spreadsheet, select the cells you'd like to merge and then click the **Merge** icon in the toolbar.

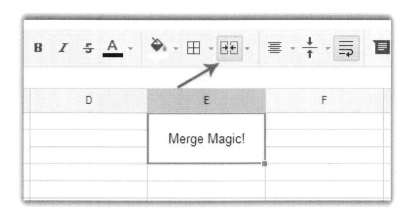

Also you can click on the Merge drop-down and select from the following options:

Merge all: Merge all selected cells into one cell.

Merge horizontally: Select this option to merge the cells in each selected row.

Merge vertically: Select this option to merge the cells in each selected column.

Unmerge: Unmerges selected cell.

Bonus Tip: After merging cells, it's a good idea to center align it. To do this, click on the Horizontal align icon and center it, and then click on the Vertical align icon and click on Middle. The same alignment is applied to the cell in the above screenshot.

How to Insert a Chart in a Spreadsheet

This may look complex but believe me, inserting a chart in a spreadsheet is a piece of cake. You can easily create, edit and customize your chart in a jiffy. To insert a chart, select that range of cells that includes your chart data and then go to **Insert > Chart** from the toolbar.

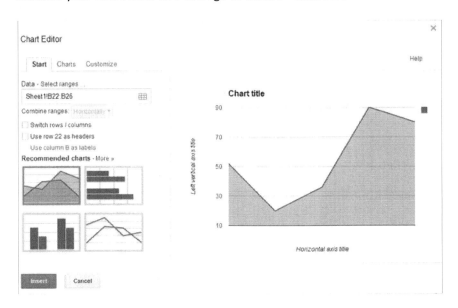

In the "Start" tab of the charts dialog box, you can edit the data range you'd like to display in your chart and preview recommended chart types. Charts are recommended based on your selected data range. In this tab, you can also swap rows with columns and mark the first column and/or row as labels for the created chart.

The "Chart" tab displays all the available chart types which can preview your data in various ways. If your data format doesn't match the required data format for a particular chart type, then spreadsheet will notify you about this with a message.

Lastly, the "Customize" tab allows you to customize your chart. You can add a title to your chart, change the legend's position, change colors, fonts and more.

Once you've completed these settings, click on the "Insert" button to insert the chart to your spreadsheet.

You can now move the chart to your preferred position by simple drag and drop. When you hover over the chart, your cursor changes to a hand type icon which means that you can now drag and drop the chart to a different position.

Now, whenever you change the data that's selected in the graph, the graph will automatically be updated. You won't need to do anything manually to update the chart.

To customize the chart, click on it and then on pencil icon to enable quick edit mode. Next, click on the area of the chart you want to edit.

Sorting and Filtering Data in Spreadsheet

Two of the most powerful features of spreadsheet are sorting and filtering. Both of these options are very useful, and can't be ignored.

Sorting:

Sorting, as the name suggests allows you to sort a range of cells. This sorting can be done according to rules set for one or more columns. To sort, follow below instructions.

1. Highlight the group of cells that you'd like to sort. If you want to sort the entire sheet, click on the top left corner of the sheet to select all cells or press Ctrl + A.
2. From the Data menu, select "Sort range."
3. Check "Data has header row" if your columns have titles.
4. Select whether you would like the column to be sorted in ascending or descending order. Click on "+Add another sort column" if you'd like to add another sorting rule. Sorting will always be prioritized according to the order of your rules. Once done, click on the "Sort" button.

Tip: If you've got a really large spreadsheet with first row as its heading, then you can freeze that row so that it's still visible even when you scroll down. This is very useful to keep the headings intact. To freeze rows or columns, go to View > Freeze rows if you want to freeze rows or "Freeze columns" if you want to freeze columns. You can freeze up to first 10 rows and first 5 columns.

Filtering:

The filter feature in spreadsheet allows you to view your data by hiding the data that you temporarily want to take out of view. This is a very useful feature if your spreadsheet is large and stuffed with data. When you want to view all your data again, simply disable the filter.

To enable filter, follow below instructions.

1. Select the range of cells you'd like to apply the filter to.
2. From the toolbar, click on the "Filter" icon. Alternatively, you can go to the Data menu and click on Filter.
3. Once you do this, the filter will be applied to your selected range of cells.
4. To help you see what cell ranges have a filter applied, the column and row labels are colored green. The filter icon on the toolbar will also change to green color.
5. Once you've enabled the filter, click on the drop down icon in the header row to view a set of filtering options. You can now check and uncheck individual data points that you want to view or filter out. Click on OK button to apply the filter. Note that you can apply only one filter per spreadsheet in order to prevent collaborators from overwriting each other's data.

You also have the ability to search for particular data points within a column that has a filter applied. Typing "J," for example, will shorten the list to just the names that start with J. You can click on "Select all" or "Clear" to perform bulk options on the visible items. For example, if you get the results of Josh and Johnny, then clicking on Select all will select both the entries whereas clicking on Clear will deselect (or clear) both the entries.

To disable filter, simply click on the filter icon from the toolbar. The filter will be removed from your selected range of cells and all filtered rows will become visible again.

How to Sort Data with Filter Enabled

You can also sort data with filter enabled. To sort, after clicking on the drop-down menu, click on either Sort A-Z or Sort Z-A. Note that only the data contained in the filter will be sorted.

How to Publish and Embed a Spreadsheet in a Webpage

When you are done creating and editing your spreadsheet, you can then publish it to a webpage. By publishing it, you will be making the file available for others to view, but they won't be able to edit or make any changes to it, and that's why, one should not confuse this with sharing.

To publish, go to the FIle menu and select "Publish to the Web." From the drop-down, select the sheet that you want to publish and then click on "Start Publishing." It makes sense to check mark "Automatically republish when changes are made."

Once you do this, you'll be able to see a link to the published data. Copy that link and then send it to your friends, family, colleagues. They can enter this URL in their browser's address bar and view the spreadsheet.

Embedding a Spreadsheet to a Website

To embed a spreadsheet, you first need to publish it by following the above steps. Once you've published the spreadsheet, go to File menu and select Publish to the Web.

From the Web page drop-down menu, click on "HTML to embed in a page." Next, grab that code and paste it in your website.

Keyboard Shortcuts for Google Spreadsheet

Moving within a sheet

Shortcut	Action
Arrow keys	Move one cell up, down, left or right
Tab	Move one cell to the right
Shift + Tab	Move one cell to the left
Home	Move to the beginning of the row
End	Move to the end of the row
Ctrl + End	Move to the last cell of the spreadsheet
Ctrl + Home	Move to the beginning of the spreadsheet
Ctrl + Left arrow/Right arrow	Go to the left most / right most of the current row
Ctrl + Up arrow/Down arrow	Go to the top most / bottom most cell of the current column
Ctrl + Shift + Page Up / Page Down	Switch between sheets

Formatting related

Shortcut	Action
Ctrl + B	Bold
Ctrl + U	Underline
Ctrl + I	Italic
Alt + Shift + 5	Strikethrough
Alt + Shift + 7	Apply outer border
Alt + Shift + 6	Remove borders
Alt + Shift + 1	Apply top border
Alt + Shift + 3	Apply bottom border
Alt + Shift + 4	Apply left border
Alt + Shift + 2	Apply right border
Ctrl + Shift + 4	Format as currency
Ctrl + Shift + 5	Format as percentage
Ctrl + Shift + 6	Format as exponent
Ctrl + Shift + 3	Format as date

Ctrl + Shift + 2	Format as time
Ctrl + Shift + 1	Format as decimal

Selection related

Shortcut	Action
Ctrl + Space	Select column
Shift + Space	Select row
Ctrl + Shift Space or Ctrl + A	Select all

Editing related

Shortcut	Action
Ctrl + Z	Undo
Ctrl + Y	Redo
Ctrl + Shift + :	Insert time
Ctrl + ;	Insert date
Ctrl + Enter	Fill range
Ctrl + D	Fill down
Ctrl + R	Fill right
Shift + F2	Insert / edit comment
F2 or Enter	Edit a cell (Fn + F2 on Mac)

Menus

Shortcut	Action
Ctrl + Shift + \	Show context menu
Alt + Shift + K	Show sheet list
Alt + Shift + S	Display sheet menu

File commands

Shortcut	Action
Ctrl + S	Save*
Ctrl + O	Open
Ctrl + Shift + S	Make a copy
Ctrl + P	Print
Shift + F11	Add new sheet

*Even if you don't press the shortcut key, Spreadsheet will still auto-save the file every few seconds.

Chapter 7: Forms

Google Forms is a very useful tool to help you do many things, for example, you can create a survey in Google Forms and send it to others, prepare a quiz, plan events, get feedback for your product or service or collect any other information from others in a simple and easy way.

Google form can also be connected to a Google spreadsheet. If a spreadsheet is linked to the form, responses will automatically be sent to the spreadsheet. Otherwise, users can view them on the "Summary of Responses" page accessible from the Responses menu.

Google Forms Toolbar Explained

Let's take a closer look at all the buttons in the Google Forms toolbar.

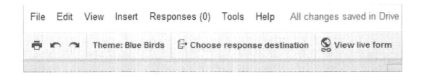

Print: Prints the document.

Undo: Undo the last action.

Redo: Redo the last action.

Theme: Change theme from here.

Choose response destination: This button allows you to choose your response destination. You can record response destination in a separate spreadsheet, new sheet but in an existing spreadsheet, or you can keep the responses only in Forms and not record in any spreadsheet.

View live form: Click on this button to view a live preview of the form

.

How to Create a Form from Google Drive or from Google Spreadsheet

How to create a form from your Google Drive account

1. Click on the red "Create" button from Google Drive's web interface and then on "Form."
2. Next, enter a title and select a theme. Select the default form if you're not happy with fancy themes.
3. Now you can start creating your form. Enter a title, description, question title, help text and question type. Click on "Add Item" to add item to your form. Same way, you can add several questions to your form by selecting different question type.

4. When you're done creating the form, click on the blue "Send form" button and then copy the link and send it to those who you wish should respond to the form. If you're creating a survey, you can post this link to your social networks or manually email the links to them.
5. Naturally, you would like to know the responses to your form/survey. You can view all the responses by clicking on "View responses" button from the toolbar, and also from Responses menu and clicking on "View responses."

How to Create a form from a Google Spreadsheet

1. To create a form from a Google spreadsheet, click on the Insert menu and select "Form".
2. A message will display at the top of the page notifying you that a new form has been created.
3. From this message, click on "Add questions here" to begin editing your form, or "Dismiss" to get rid of this message and continue editing your spreadsheet.
4. Just in case if you dismiss this message, then you can edit the form at any time from Form menu and selecting "Edit form."
5. Once you do this, you'll notice a new tab at the bottom of your spreadsheet labeled "Form responses." This is where responses to your form will be added.

How to Add Section Heading, Images and Page Break to a Form

It is a good idea to properly format the form and divide your questions in various sections. You wouldn't like your form to look complicated enough which would make respondents close your form right away. Ideally you should divide your form in different pages. Let's learn how to add section headings, page breaks and images to a form.

To add a section header, page break and image, go to the **Insert menu** and click on the respective option.

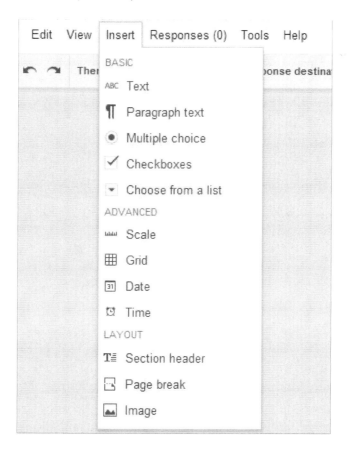

Page break: Page breaks are very useful if your form is lengthy. If you would just list out all the questions in one place then you might scare the respondents, and that's why, it is essential to break the form into several pages. That's why, you should definitely use page break option and list out a few questions on each page.

Section header: Section header can help you divide the form into sections so that it is easier to read and complete. This option basically lets you add a heading and a description for your next section.

Image: As they say, a picture says a thousand words. If you want to make your form more interesting, then you can insert images to it. Once you've uploaded an image, you can specify the image title and text that will appear when someone hovers over the image.

The Insert menu allows you to insert many other elements like text, paragraph text, multiple choice, checkboxes, choose from a list, scale, grid, date and time.

Chapter 8: Drawing

Google Drawing enables you to easily create, edit and share drawings online. Think of this as an alternative to Microsoft's Paint but with different set of features.

Here are some of the features of Drawing:

- Edit drawings online in real time with anyone you choose, and invite others to view your edits in real time.
- Chat with others who are editing your drawing, from within the drawings editor.
- Publish drawings online to the world as images, or download them in standard formats.
- Insert text, shapes, arrows, scribbles, and images from your hard drive or from the Web.
- Lay out drawings precisely with alignment guides, snap to grid, and auto distribution.
- Insert drawings into other Google documents, spreadsheets, or presentations using the web clipboard, then tweak them inline.

Drawing is so simple and easy to learn that you'd be surprised. There are no complicated options, and of course, one should not think of Drawing as an alternative to Photoshop. Let's proceed to the next chapter and learn how to create a drawing.

How to Create, Edit and Insert New Elements to Drawing

To create a new Drawing, go to Google Drive's web interface and click on the red "Create" button and select "Drawing."

You can now start creating your next master piece!

Toolbar Explained

Before we move forward with the advanced stuff, let's learn about the toolbar.

Undo: Undo the last action.

Redo: Redo the last action.

Paint format: Apply the same formatting to a different element with this tool.

Zoom to fit: If you've zoomed-in, then use this button to fit the drawing on the screen.

Zoom: Zoom in.

Select: Select any element with this button.

Line: Add a line to the drawing. Click on the small drop-down menu next to it to draw arrow, curve, polyline, arc and scribble.

Shape: Add shapes, arrows, callouts and equation.

Text box: Add a text box.

Image: Insert an image to the drawing. You can select an image either from your Google Drive account or by manually uploading an image from your computer.

Insert comment: Insert a comment to the drawing.

How to Insert Text box, Image, Wordart, Shapes, Table and more in Drawing

You can use the Insert menu to insert various elements in Drawing. Apart from that, you can also use the Toolbar to insert line, shapes, text box, image and comment.

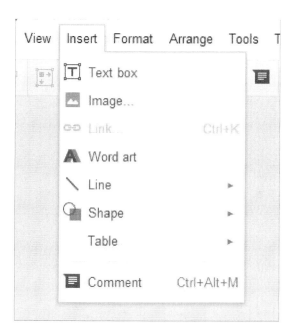

Text box: Inserts a text box to the Drawing. You can click and drag the mouse to define the text area.

Image: Inserts an image from your Google Drive account or you can also manually upload an image from your computer.

Link: Inserts a hyperlink to a web address or an email address. You need to first select a text or an object and then you can add a hyperlink to that element.

Wordart: After selecting this option, type your text and press Enter.

Line: Click to place one end of the line and then drag it to the other end. Press Shift and then drag it to make a straight line. Note that in line, arrow, and scribble modes, you'll keep adding lines until you go back to select mode by clicking the Select button from the toolbar or pressing Esc.

Shape: Shape lets you insert various shapes like arrows, callouts and equations. Click on your desired shape and then drag it to the other end.

Table: Add table to your drawing with this option.

Comment: Adds comment to your drawing.

How to Edit an Element

To edit an element, simply select it first and then go to the Edit menu to cut, copy, paste, delete and duplicate the element.

For some shapes, you'll get additional options in the Toolbar which lets you perform more actions on that particular selected object.

For Wordart, you just need to double-click on it and then start editing it.

Apply Formatting to your Drawing

After inserting objects, you can format them using the buttons in the toolbar. For example, when you select a shape, Fill color, Line color, Line width, Dashes, and Edit Text buttons appear.

Fill color: Use this button to fill color to the entire selected object.

To increase or decrease transparency, click on Fill color and then choose "Custom." Next, drag the opacity selector down to increase an object's transparency, while dragging up decreases transparency.

To apply a background to your entire drawing page, right-click in the canvas, select "Background" and choose your desired color.

To change the color of a shape's border, click on the "Line color" button and then select your preferred color. To change the thickness of the border, click on "Line width" button.

To modify the style of a shape's border, click on the "Dashes" button and then apply a new style to your border.

Useful Keyboard Modifiers

You can use keyboard modifiers when performing actions to take advantage of various useful features.

Turn off guides or snap to grid: Hold down the Alt key when dragging an object.

To preserve an object's aspect ratio when resizing, hold down the Shift key when resizing an object.

To rotate an object in 15 degree increments, hold down the Shift key when resizing an object.

To duplicate an object, hold down Ctrl key when moving an object. The original object will be left in its place and a new duplicate object will be created.

Select, Align, Group and Ungroup Objects in Drawing

To select all objects in the Drawing, press Ctrl + A. To select multiple objects, press the Shift key and then click on objects to select them. To deselect a particular object, press the Ctrl key.

After selecting multiple objects, you can align them in a variety of ways from Arrange > Align horizontally / Align vertically. You can also center all the selected elements on the page from Arrange > Center on page and then select whether you want to arrange horizontally or vertically.

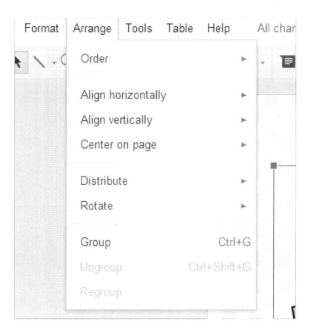

Once you select multiple objects, you can Group them. When objects are grouped, you can manipulate all of the objects in the group as if they were a single object. All of the actions that can be performed on a single object can then be done to all objects in the group at the same time. This means that you won't need to select all those objects every time you want to perform an action. To Group objects, select all the objects that you want to group and then go to Arrange > Group or press Ctrl + G shortcut key. To ungroup, simply press Ctrl + Shift + G.

How to Download Drawing file as JPG, PNG & Other Formats

So you finally created your master piece using Drawing and now you want to download that to your computer. The good part is that Drawing allows you to download the file as PDF document (.PDF), Scalable Vector Graphics (.SVG), PNG image (.PNG) and JPEG image (.JPG) formats.

Go to File menu > Download as and then select your preferred format.

Tip: Download the image as PNG if you want to download the image without any background. Of course if you've filled a color in the background, then the background would not be transparent.

Chapter 9: Sharing / Collaboration

One of the plus point or feature that really stands out in Google Drive is the sharing and collaboration. You can share your Google Documents, Presentations, Spreadsheet, Form and Drawing with anyone. You can also share other PDFs, images, videos, etc with others just like you do with other cloud storage services but first, let's focus on how sharing works in Google Docs.

How to Share a Document with Other People

You can share your Google Document with your friends, family, or coworkers. You can do this from your Drive or directly from the document.

- Method 1: From your Google Drive's web interface, select the document you want to share (you can also select multiple documents), and then click on the Share button.

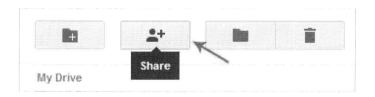

- Method 2: If you want to share any open document, then click on the blue Share button located at the top right of the window.

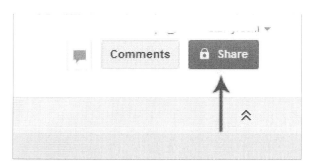

The same method can be applied to share any Presentation, Spreadsheet or any other Google document.

Next, follow the below steps:

1. Under "Invite people," type the email addresses of people you want to share your document with. You can add a single person or an entire mailing list.
2. To the right of the list of names, select "Can view," "Can edit," or "Can comment" from the drop-down menu. Please don't skip this step as it is very important that you give correct permission to the person that you're inviting.
3. If you'd like to add a message to your invitation, click "Add message" and enter some text.

4. Click **"Share & save."** By default, an email will be sent to the person whom you are inviting, but if you don't want to do this then uncheck the option "Notify the people via email." You can also get the "Link to Share" to copy the link and share it with others.

From the same window, you can see who has access to the document; you can also change the type of access, or remove editors, commenters, and viewers, and change your document's visibility option.

If you would like to manually share the link to your collaborator, then copy the link from "Link to share" and send it to your collaborators.

Click on "Change" and then you can change the visibility options for the document. For example; you can make it public, you can set it such that anyone with a link can access your file, or let it remain private.

Note that if the file is made public, then anyone on the internet can find and access your file. Sign-in wouldn't be required for such a file.

Send or Share the File as Email Attachment

The above method displays how to share a file in Drive. It will also automatically notify the person to whom you've been sharing the file via an email. There's no need to send files as email attachments, but still if you prefer to do this, then simply follow the below procedure:

1. Open the file that you want to share.
2. Go to the File menu and select "Email as attachment."

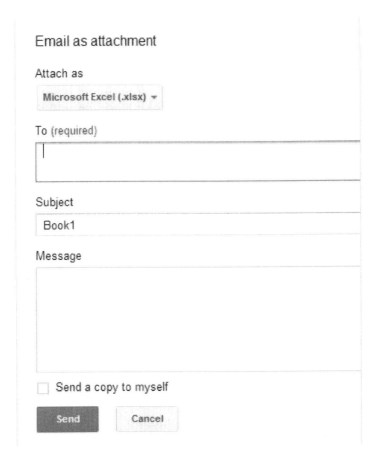

3. In the "Attach as" drop-down menu, select the file type.
4. In the "To" field, enter the email address, add a subject and a message. Once done, click on the "Send" button.

The recipient will receive the file as a downloadable attachment in the format you've selected.

Another way to do the same thing is to first download the file in your preferred format from File -> Download as. Next, you can then attach the same file in an email and send it.

Tips for Sharing a File in Google Drive

Share files only with people who you trust:

Sharing a file in Google Drive is easy, but you should share it only with those people whom you trust. You wouldn't want your confidential information to leak online, or you wouldn't want anyone to delete some important data from the spreadsheet or document. That's why, when you share the file, from the "Can edit" drop-down, make sure what rights you're giving to the collaborator. That's why; think before you give editing and commenting rights to the collaborator.

Notify people when you share the file:

When you share the file, ensure that you check mark "Notify people via email." This setting means that the person whom you're sharing the file with will receive an email notification letting them know that you're sharing the file with them. The next time they'll login to their Google Drive account, they'll have access to that file.

Share lots of files at once by sharing an entire folder:

If you want to share multiple items with your collaborators, move them into a folder and then share that entire folder with them. They'll be able to access whatever's stored inside that folder. To share more files with them, simply move a file into that folder and to remove a file from sharing, simply move the file out from that folder.

Create a Google Group and add lots of collaborators quickly:

If you're going to invite many collaborators, then you'll need to type their email addresses one-by-one. Instead, add an entire Google Group. Each member of that Google Group will have access to whatever you've shared, including people who are added to the group after you've shared something. Check out Google Groups https://groups.google.com/forum.

Chapter 10: Best Google Drive Apps

You can make Drive a powerhouse if you connect it to various third-party apps. When you connect Drive to these apps, you can extend the functionality of Drive and do many more things that were not possible before. Let's first learn how to connect these third-party apps to Drive.

Login to Drive on the web and click on the red "Create" button and then on "Connect more apps."

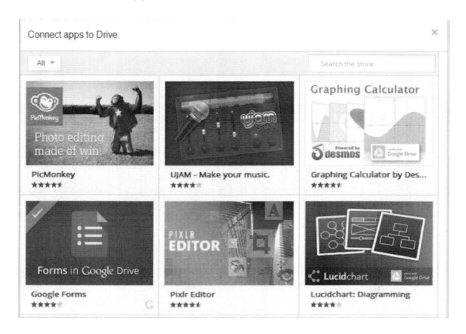

This will open the Connect apps to Drive window. From here, you can connect any of the apps to your Drive. But one question that would come to your mind is: Which apps are worth using from all this? That's why, let's take a look at some of the most useful Drive apps that you can use right now.

Tip: In the search box, enter the name of the below apps and search for it. There's no need to scroll over the entire list manually. Once you find the app that you're looking for, click on the "Connect" button. Some apps will add their shortcuts to the create button so that they can be launched instantly.

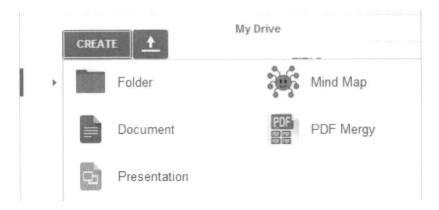

MindMup

MindMup is a free online mind mapping tool. It lets you create mind-maps easily and in the most simplest way ever possible. Once you connect this app with your Drive, it creates a shortcut. Click on the red Create button and then on Mind Map to start creating your mind map.

Your MindMup mind-maps are automatically saved to Google Drive as a .mup file and will be synced to your computer, smartphone and tablet apps via your Google Drive application. The app also supports Freemind mind map import/export.

Drive Notepad

Drive Notepad lets you view and edit all kinds of text documents in your browser. It also comes with syntax highlighting for many scripting and programming languages. Files created using this app are stored in your Drive account, and if you're on Windows, then you can open those files in Notepad. Since Drive doesn't comes with any app that lets you create plain text files, this app lets you do just that, and in a very simple way.

HelloSign

Do you believe in paperless office? How about signing your documents digitally? HelloSign is a new way to sign the documents. Simply open your file, add a signature (or text, date, checkmark, etc.) and let HelloSign do the rest. It's legally binding and takes less than a minute. Integrate Google Drive & HelloSign and you'll be on your way to a paperless office.

When you sync HelloSign to Google Drive it will add a HelloSign folder to your Drive homepage. All copies of sent and received documents will be stored here for your convenience, which means you won't have to go back to the website to access them.

Floorplanner

With Floorplanner, you can create beautiful floor plans. If you're moving into a new house, planning a wedding, or re-organizing your living room, Floorplanner has the right tools for you. With Floorplanner you can recreate your home, garden or office in just a few clicks and furnish your plans with huge library of objects.

This tool may not be perfect for architects and interior designers, but for the average person who's looking to design their next home design plan, it's perfect for him. When you're done, files are saved in Drive and then accessible from any browser with just a click.

HelloFax

HelloFax lets you sign documents and send faxes online. When you first signup, HelloFax gives you some free fax pages which should be enough to get started. After connecting the app with your Drive, you can then start sending the document to a fax machine by right-clicking on it, and selecting HelloFax under "Open with" menu. You'll of course need to add a fax number after that. If someone replies, or sends you a fax, that fax will be forwarded to your email as a PDF. You never have to touch a fax machine or spend any money on it.

PicMonkey

Want to edit photos but without any complicated tools? Then PicMonkey is what you should try. To edit a photo with PicMonkey, once you've connected the app, right-click on any supported image file and then go to Open with > PicMonkey.

PicMonkey has features like Collage, Touch Up, Teeth Whiten, Fonts, Effects, Filters, Frames, Stickers & more.

WeVideo

WeVideo is an online video editor. It offers three video editing modes – Storyboard, Timeline and Advanced mode. You can trim video clips, split long clips and rearrange them, enter text in the video, record voice overs, add effects, music transition and do much more. The app connects with Facebook, Instagram, Flickr, Google Drive & Dropbox to easily use photos, videos, music & graphics files that are already uploaded. Once you're ready, you can save the video and all its assets to a single folder in Google Drive which you can access from anywhere. Videos can fill up your space really fast and that's why, you may like to delete any files that you're not going to use.

DriveTunes

Want to play music/songs/audio directly from your Google Drive? Then DriveTunes is what you should try. DriveTunes allows you to play mp3 and m4a audio files right from Google Drive. With this app, you can queue and listen to music in Drive, rather than just previewing it. The app allows you to search through all songs, order songs by title or number of plays, or you can also play from some specific folders.

PDF Mergy

PDF Mergy allows you to merge PDF files with a simple drag and drop interface. You can either upload your PDF files from your computer or select a file from your Drive. Once you've selected two or more PDF files, you can then drag and drop them to bring in the desired order. When you're done, you can hit the Merge button. The merged file can then be saved to your computer or Drive. However, in order to process your files, they will be uploaded to a remote server. Therefore, you should not use it with confidential files. Apart from that, it works great in doing the task of merging PDF files, and that too, using Drive.

Gantter for Google Drive

Gantter is an enterprise cloud-based project scheduling solution integrated with Google Drive. Gantter features all the power of leading desktop scheduling software products without users having to buy or install anything. It also allows you to easily import and open your existing Microsoft Project files.

PDFUnlock

As the name suggests, PDFUnlock removes restrictions and password from PDF files. You just need to select the file that you wish to unlock and then hit the Unlock button. You can then download the unlocked PDF to your computer.

DriveConverter

DriveConverter is a file converter for files that are stored in your Google Drive. It supports converting to many different formats like PDF, XML, DOC, DOCX, XLSX, PNG, JPG, HTML, TXT, and more. Once DriveConverter is added to Chrome, right click on any of the supported files in Google Drive and select Open With > DriveConverter. Next, you have to simply follow the instructions to convert the file.

You can discover more apps that work with Drive from "Connect more apps" itself.

Chapter 11: Best Add-ons for Google Docs and Sheets

Add-ons are something that adds more advanced functionality to your Docs and Sheets. Think of this as much similar to apps, but add-ons are integrated in Docs and Sheets. You can access various add-ons by clicking on "Add-ons" from the menu bar. Note that at the time of writing this, add-ons are only available for Docs and Sheets.

Once you go to Add-ons menu and click on "Get Add-ons" and then you will be able to browse all the available add-ons. To install an add-on, click on the "Free" button. You'll then need to grant permission to that add-on by clicking on the "Accept" button. Once the add-on is installed, it can be accessed from the same add-on menu. For example, here's how it looks like after installing two add-ons in Docs.

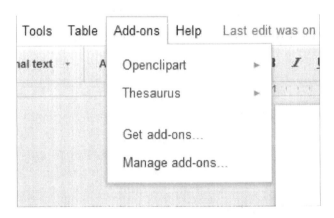

Since there are so many add-ons, let's take a look at some popular and useful add-ons for **Google Docs**:

Track Changes: Microsoft Word comes with a superb Track Changes feature. This add-on lets you bring the same functionality to Google Docs. You can also selectively track changes you like, and discard the ones that you don't.

Thesaurus: Thesaurus for Google Documents revolutionizes your experience by helping you explore synonyms, antonyms and more.

Gliffy Diagrams: Create professional-looking diagrams quickly and easily in Google Docs. Draw flowcharts, wireframes, UML, ERD and more.

Consistency Checker: How would you ensure that you're having the same consistency in the entire document? This Consistency Checker add-on is intended for long or formal documents where consistency is hard to maintain. If you're creating a formal document, then this add-on is surely giving worth a try at.

EasyBib Bibliography Creator: This add-on helps you to easily add bibliography and citation to Google Docs. It lets you automatically cite books, journal articles, and websites just by entering in the titles or URLs.

DocumentMerge: This add-on produces multiple documents from a single template and data from Google Spreadsheet. With this add-on you can quickly and easily merge the data from your spreadsheets to flow into your Google Docs, allowing you to quickly process and create documents that would normally take hours to make.

Translate: This add-on allows you to quickly translate selected document text between several languages and reinsert it into the document.

Now let's take a look at some useful add-ons for **Google Sheets**:

Styles: This add-on lets you quickly add style to your spreadsheet by highlighting cells and choosing a style from the style viewer. Give a more colorful look to your boring spreadsheets with this add-on.

Mapping Sheets: This add-on provides an easy way to plot your data onto a Google Map directly from Google Sheets with just a few clicks. Plus, when viewing your data on the Google Map, you will have access to the fastest searching and filtering tools available.

Template Gallery: This add-on lets you quickly add ready-made templates to your sheets. Browse a large gallery of professionally designed templates, including calendars, schedules, invoices, time sheets, budgeting tools, letters, resumes, financial calculators, and more.

Advanced Find and Replace: This add-on extends the basic find and replace functionality of Sheets. It will help you complete any substitutions in your sheets in seconds. With this add-on, you can search in values, formulas, notes, hyperlinks in all sheets at once.

More Fonts: Ever wished that you could use more fonts apart from the six default font offering? Then this add-on is for you. It adds 35 popular fonts to your Sheets.

Remove Duplicates: This add-on comes with two useful wizards. One will help you compare two different tables and remove duplicates; the other will search for unique and duplicate rows within one sheet. This is a superb add-on to quickly find duplicates and remove them.

Yet Another Mail Merge: Create your mail template as a draft in Gmail and merge it with your Sheet data.

Chapter 12: Useful Tips and Tricks for Google Drive

Let's take a look at some useful tips and tricks that will help you to get the most out of Google Drive and Docs. You wouldn't want to miss them!

How to Revert Back to an Old Version of a Google Docs File

Thankfully, Google Drive comes with an auto-save feature which means you don't need to click on any save button, unlike other office suites. This means that you don't need to worry about power loss or accidentally closing it. In Google Drive, your document is automatically saved every few seconds. The same is true for Gmail, as it too auto-saves the email as you write.

The best part about Google Drive is that it automatically saves your document revision history which means that you can always revert back to old version of any Google Docs file. To open Revision History, simply follow below steps:

1. Open your Google document, spreadsheet or presentation.
2. Go to File -> See revision history (shortcut key is Ctrl+Alt+Shift+G).
3. This will open the revision history pain the right side of the browser screen, with a list of all the saved revisions, along with date, time and people who made the changes.

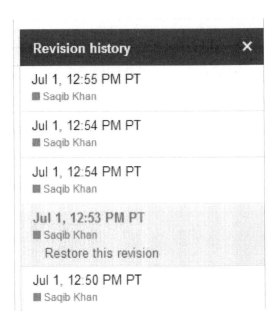

4. Select an earlier version to view it on the screen. Don't worry, simply selecting it won't restore to that version.

5. If you would like to restore to an old version, then click on "Restore this revision".

6. To go back to the most recent version, click at the top most revision and restore it.

Note that Google says that they'll automatically delete old versions after 30 days or 100 revisions. Apart from that, the revision history feature of Google Docs works great.

Quickest Way to Delete Doc, Slide or Sheet that You've Been Working On

Many of us use Docs, Slide or Sheet as an instant editor for quick tasks. This means that if you quickly want to note down something important, let's say name, address and phone number, then you would open Doc and enter all the information there temporarily. The only problem with this is that this behavior would leave us with many semi-finished items in Drive. Once you've noted down your information, you would then need to trash that file manually.

Now, the good thing is that Google Drive now allows you to quickly delete the file that you've been working on. You can quickly delete Doc, Slide or Sheet without going back to Drive's main interface.

To delete a file that you've been working on, go to the File menu and click on "Move to Trash." Note that if you do this, then the file would be sent to the Trash folder instantly.

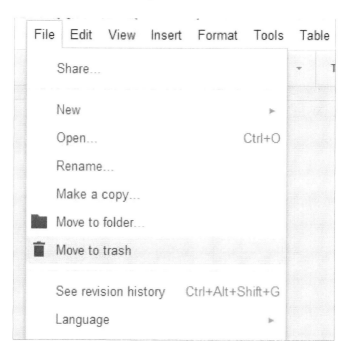

If you want to delete it permanently, then you'll need to go to the Trash folder and delete it from there. Just in case if you want to restore it, then you can do so by going to Trash, selecting the file and then clicking on "Restore" button.

Fastest Way to Save Online Images, Documents, PDFs or Links Directly to Drive

How would you share or store an image or document that you found online with others? Normally, you would first download the image or document and then upload it to your Drive. This process is not that long but it's not convenient when you want to regularly upload large files to your Drive account.

That's where you can use a Chrome extension named as Ballloon (yes, there are three L's in the name). This extension eliminates the downloading process, as all you'll need to do is one simple left click on the image and the file will be uploaded to the cloud.

As always, head over to the Chrome web store to install the extension. Click on the Free button and then click on "Add" to install this extension.

Once installed, you would notice a small new Ballloon icon on the Chrome toolbar. Click on this icon and then sign-in to your Google account.

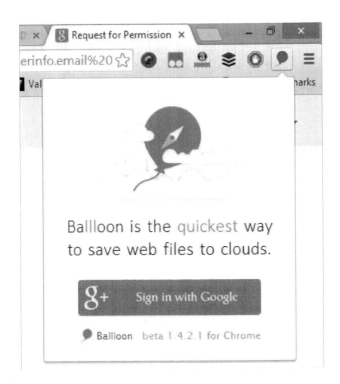

Ballloon is the quickest way to save web files to clouds.

8+ Sign in with Google

Ballloon beta 1.4.2.1 for Chrome

On the next page, click on "Accept" button to grant permission to this app to create files in your Drive account.

Now, visit any website and hover over an image. You'll be able to see a small overlay at the top right of the image with the buttons for Dropbox and Google Drive. Click on the Drive icon. The first time you use either option, you need to authorize Balllon's access, but once you do this, from then onwards it would be a simple one-click process.

Same way, you can also save documents, PDFs and links. To save links, right-click on it and then go to Save link to > Google Drive.

Everything that you save using Ballloon is saved to a separate Ballloon folder. From there, they're ready to share with other people, or to access on another computer.

Ballloon surely is the simplest and fastest way to save web files directly to Drive and Dropbox. As per their website, support for OneDrive and Box is coming soon.

Visit the official website of this extension from http://ballloon.com.

Save Web Clips to Google Drive Using Piconka

If you've ever used Evernote's web clipper extension, then you know how saving web clips work.   But if you're searching for something that works with your Drive account too, then look no further. Piconka is a web clipper that has a minimalist approach, and it saves your web clips directly to your Drive account. This means Piconka will never have access to your saved stuff, as all it does is to save web clips and send it to Drive.

Here's how it works. Head over to Chrome web store and then install the extension. Once installed, head over to Piconka.com, sign-in and then authorize it so that it can save stuff to your Drive account.

Welcome!

Connect your Google Drive account

Use Google Drive to save bookmarks. We protect your confidentiality - Piconka won't view or have access to your data.

Connect to Google Drive

Once authorized, you can start using it. Now, open a web page and simply select a text or an image with your mouse and then drag it to the center of your screen. You'll now notice a small green + box. Drop your selected data into it and you're done.

To view all your clips, click on the Piconka icon on the toolbar which will open a pane on the right side. From there, you can also delete, share, or add a tag to your web clip.

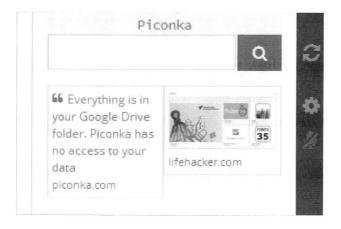

All the clips are saved into your Drive account in a separate "Piconka" folder. However, you can also create a new folder from the web interface.

So go ahead, instead of using the traditional bookmarks method, try using this new method to save stuff from the web.

5 Useful Tips to Secure your Google Drive

Of course Google Drive is secure even without doing anything, but there are always ways to further strengthen your Drive account. Let's take a look at 4 tips which you can apply right now to secure your Google Drive account (and yes, they're worth trying out).

Tip #1: Enable Two-Step Verification

As we all know, our login credentials are the most important thing in this online world. If a hacker has guessed your email and password, then he can access not only your Google Drive account but can also access all Google apps and services. That's why; it is a good idea to enable two-step verification to secure your Google account.

Once you enable two-step verification, you'll not only need to enter your password but also a second code that Google sends to your mobile phone via text message. If someone tries to hack your account, they'll need not only your password but also your phone which would be impossible to obtain.

There are two ways to receive the verification on your mobile phone:

1. Via text messages.
2. If you're using an Android smartphone then you can install the Google Authenticator app to get your verification code.

To enable two-step verification, visit https://www.google.com/accounts/SmsAuthConfig and then follow the on-screen instructions..

Tip #2: Revoke App's Permission to Specific Files

In Google Drive we store variety of files, from office documents, taxes and invoices to what not. It is a central place for important files and that's why it makes sense to protect some of those precious files. When you grant certain apps access to your Google Drive, you're allowing those apps to access your files, and if you want to protect certain important files then it is a good idea to revoke app's permission to those certain files.

For example; let's say you don't want any app to access your invoice file. To do this, simply right-click on that file and select "View authorized apps."

Rename...
Mark as unviewed
View authorized apps...
Make a copy

Next, click on the revoke button next to any app that you don't want to give access to. Don't worry, you'll still have access to your file but the app won't be able to access your file anymore.

Tip #3: Revoke App's Access to your Entire Drive

The above tip works great if you want to remove certain files from being accessed by any app, but what if you don't want that app to access your Drive at all? If you're not using any apps that you've authorized then it is a good idea to revoke app's access to your account.

To do this, go to https://www.google.com/settings/account and click on "Security" from the left. Scroll down and click on "Review permissions."

You'll now see a page which lists out all the apps and services that you've authorized till date. Simply click on "Revoke access" button and you're done.

> ## Authorized Access to your Google Account
>
> ### Connected Sites, Apps, and Services
>
> You have granted the following services access to your Google Account:
>
> Google Drive — Google Contacts, Google Contacts, Full Account Access, G
>
> Google Chrome — Full Account Access [Revoke Access]
>
> Google Drive — Google Talk [Revoke Access]

Once you click on the button, you'll get a confirmation message that says that you've successfully revoked access to that app or service.

Tip #4: Configure Recovery Options for your Account

It can happen that you forgot your password and you're unable to login to your account. In such a case, if you've configured recovery option then you'll still be able to access your account. Also these recovery options help secure your account from hackers and gives access to the rightful owner.

Visit the account recovery option page from https://security.google.com/settings/security?ref=home and ensure that you've already added a recovery email address, mobile phone number and a security question. And of course, make sure that you remember these details as you'll need these information in case you're not able to login to your account.

Tip #5: Encrypt your Sensitive Files in Google Drive

You can store their personal and confidential files in Drive which means that even if something happens to your computer, your files are stored safely online. But if you're concerned about putting your confidential data under someone else's control then there's something that you can do about it. Before uploading the file to the cloud, simply encrypt them with a password.

This can be easily done by using a free ZIP application like 7-Zip or PeaZip. You need to simply create an archive with a password and then upload it to Drive.

How to Access Google Drive Even When You're Not Connected to the Internet

It might be possible that you're not always connected to the Internet. There might be Internet outages, long plane ride or, subways where you cannot get Internet connectivity. What would you do if you want to access Google Drive on the web in such a case? Fortunately, you can enable offline access to Google Drive so that the next time you're offline you'll still be able to view Google documents, spreadsheets, presentations, and drawings, shuffle folders around, and edit files stored in your Google Drive folder.

Before proceeding forward, note that this method works only if you're using Chrome browser or a Chrome OS device. If you're using Chrome OS, then there's no need to do anything more as offline access is already enabled for you. But if you're on Chrome browser, then follow the below steps enable offline access.

1. From Drive's online interface at drive.google.com, click on "More" from the left sidebar of the screen.
2. Click on "Offline".

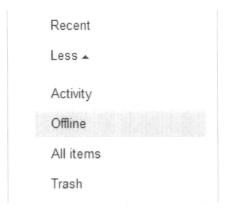

3. From here, you'll need to perform two-steps. First, click on the blue "Get the app" button. If you've already installed the app, then you won't need to do this.

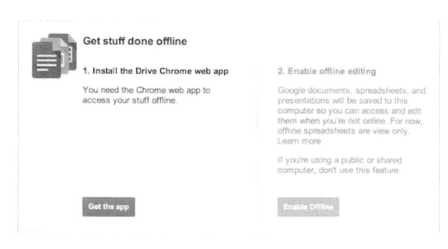

Get stuff done offline

1. Install the Drive Chrome web app

You need the Chrome web app to access your stuff offline.

2. Enable offline editing

Google documents, spreadsheets, and presentations will be saved to this computer so you can access and edit them when you're not online. For now, offline spreadsheets are view only. Learn more

If you're using a public or shared computer, don't use this feature.

Get the app

Enable Offline

4. You'll now be taken to the Chrome web store. Click on "Add to Chrome" from the upper-right corner of the screen.
5. Once the app is installed, you'll be taken to a Chrome page with the Drive icon. Return back to Drive.
6. From "More" click on Offline again and then click on "Enable Offline."

You can now view Google documents, spreadsheets, presentations, drawings, PDFs, Microsoft Office files and images even without an Internet connection. You can also edit Google documents, presentations, and drawings while offline. During offline access mode activated, you can also create new document, presentation and drawing.

When you are offline and editing a document, you'll get a message that says "All changes saved offline." This basically means that all of your changes are saved offline, and not online. When you're connected to the Internet again, you'll get a message that says "All changes saved in Drive." It means that the changes that you've made while offline are now updated online in Google Drive.

If you no longer want to access your Drive offline, click the Gear icon in the upper-right corner of your window and select "Disable Offline".

Note that only one Google account per Chrome profile can configure offline access. If you want to enable offline access for multiple Drive accounts, then you'll need to create a different Chrome profile too.

While offline access is a great feature of Google Drive, you should enable it only on your personal computer, or on a computer that you trust. Enabling offline access on public or shared computers can put your data at risk, as anyone can view your synced documents, spreadsheets and presentations.

How to Save Anything from the Web Directly to your Google Drive

When browsing on the web, sometimes you may feel the need to save images, videos, audios, PDFs, documents, and other file types to your Google Drive account. Fortunately, there's a way to save such files from the web directly to your Google Drive account using a Chrome extension. This extension eliminates the manual way to upload, which first requires you to download the file to your computer and then upload it to the Drive. It allows you to directly send the file to Google Drive.

You need to be using Chrome browser for this to work. Open Chrome Web Store and search for "Save to Google Drive" extension. Once you find the extension, click on the "Add to Chrome" button. Next, you'll be asked for confirmation and you'll need to click on "Add" button. With this step, Save to Google Drive extension is installed.

You'll now be able to see the Drive icon in your toolbar. Click on it as you'll first need to grant permission for this extension to use your account. Sign-in to your Google Drive account and click on "Grant access" button.

Now, let's say you found an interesting image on the web that you want to save to Drive. To do this, right-click on that image and then click on "Save image to Google Drive."

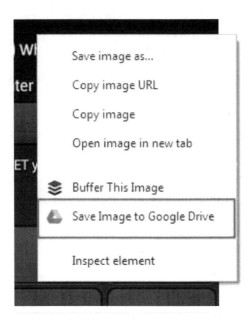

After your content is saved, the progress dialog allows you to open the file, rename, trash, or view the file in the Google Drive document list.

You can also save a particular URL to your Drive by clicking on the Drive icon from the toolbar. A screenshot will be captured and then saved in the PNG format. If you want to change this setting, then right-click on the Drive icon and then click on "Options." From here, you can change the save page setting to PNG, HTML, web archive, and Google Document.

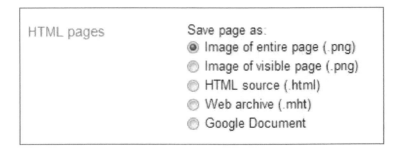

Same way, you can save many other type of files too. If the media is HTML5 video then you'll be able to see "Save Video to Google Drive"

and if the media is HTML5 audio file, then you'll be able to see "Save Audio to Google Drive" option. However, note that not all audio and video files on the web are published in HTML 5 format, which means not every audio and video file can be saved to Drive.

Overall it can be said that this extension can surely come useful if you want to quickly send any web content be it ZIP file, images, video or anything else to your Drive account. Best of all, you don't need to download it to your computer, as the extension will directly upload the file to Drive. It surely saves time!

Scan Photos or Documents with Google Drive app on your Android Phone

Do you want to scan a document or photo? Then the good thing is that there's no need for a scanner – all you need is an Android smartphone and Drive app. These days when smartphones are become smarter and powerful, your phone's camera is also capable to do many more things than just to take pictures.

With the Drive app for Android, you can scan photos, important documents, receipts, letters, and billing statements. Of course, the quality of scanned image depends on your phone's camera, and if you've got a decent camera in your phone, then you're good to go. After you've scanned a document, the app will save it as a searchable PDF file and store it right in your Drive.

Here's how to scan a document in Drive app.

1. Install and launch the Drive open on your Android phone or tablet, and tap on the three dot icon on the top right (as seen in the below screenshot) and then select "Scan."

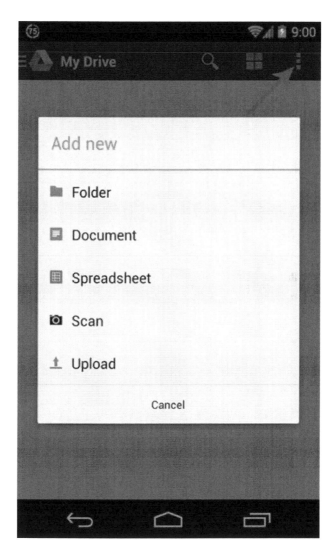

2. Point your camera at a document that you'd like to scan and click on the big scan button.

3. Drive will capture the document and then extract only the document part from the rest of the photo. It will remove the background from the document automatically.

4. From the next screen, you can rotate and crop the document before saving it to Drive. To save, tap on the tick mark button.

That's all you need to do. Your document will be saved in your Drive as a searchable PDF.

Well, you just saved yourself from buying a scanner!

Attaching Files to Gmail from Google Drive

At times, you might want to attach a file from Drive to your message.

There are two ways to attach files to a message in Gmail. You can either attach a file to a message by clicking on the "Attach files" button (paperclip icon) from the Compose window, or you can click on "Insert files using Drive" button.

If you attach the files using the paperclip icon, then you'll need to upload a file from your computer. While this works great for many, you should note that the attached file should not exceed 25MB size limit. If you'd like to send attachments larger than this, then you can insert files from Google Drive instead.

To do this, click on the Drive icon. Once you click on this button, you can either upload a new file to Drive, or click on "My Drive" to attach a file which already exists in your Drive.

Simply select a file that you want to insert and then click on "Insert" button.

To remove the attachment that you just inserted, click on "x" to the right of the file name.

Tip: You can also drag and drop attachments directly into the compose window. If the file that you're attaching is an image, then you can drop it at the big "Drop files here" to add the image inline (embed it) or drop it to "Drop to attach" section to attach the file normally.

How to Change/Remove Apps from using your Drive Account

If you're one of that adventurous type who wants to experiment with different apps, then you must have tried out many of the above apps. While there's no problem in trying out these apps, but it makes sense to remove those apps that you're not going to use. You wouldn't want many apps to access your Google account, do you? Plus many of these apps just add more clutter to your Create dialog box. That's why; let's learn how to remove apps from your account.

Step 1: Click on the Gear icon (also known as Settings button) from the top-right of Drive and then click on "Manage apps."

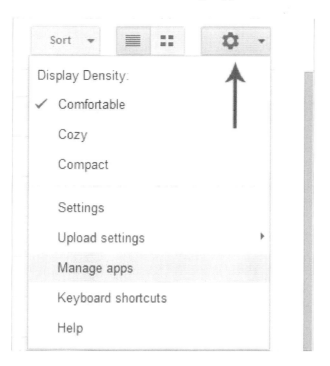

Step 2: Now you can see that for many file types, the "Use by default" option is active. If you don't want any particular app to be the default app for that file type, then simply uncheck this option. But if you want to disconnect (remove) the app from your Drive account, then click on

"Options" and then on "Disconnect from Drive." The app will now be removed from your Drive. If you want to use that app again, then you'll need to grant permission to that app again from the "connect more apps" page.

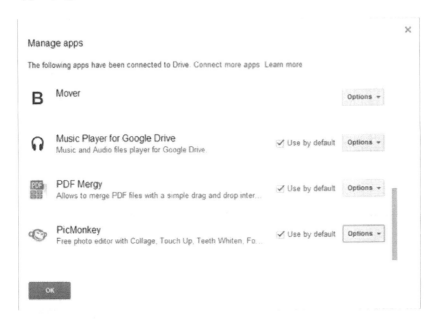

So the next time you try out an app and don't like it, you now know from where to remove it.

How to Add Google Drive to Windows Send To Menu

If you're on Windows then the only way to upload/copy files to Drive is by copying-pasting the file or folder to the Drive folder. But instead of doing this, you can simply add a Google Drive option to your right-click Send To menu. Here's how:

Step 1: First of all, you'll need to open the Send To folder. To do this, copy the following text and paste it in Run or in the search field in the Start menu. After pasting it, press Enter.

%APPDATA%/Microsoft/Windows/SendTo

Step 2: This will open the Send to folder on your computer. In your Windows Explorer, you will be able to see the Favorites folder. Right-click the Google Drive folder in your Favorites, hold down the right mouse button, and then drag and drop it to your Send To folder. Once you do this, you'll be able to see a menu. Click on "Copy here."

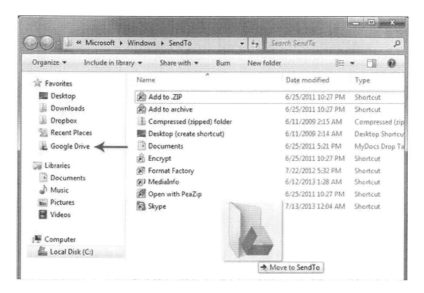

That's it. Now you'll be able to see the Google Drive folder added in your right-click Send To menu.

Now whenever you want to send any file or folder to your Drive, right-click on it > Send To and select Google Drive. That file will be copied to your Drive. This eliminates the manual process which required you to first copy the file and then paste it by navigating to the Drive folder.

Empty the Trash to Get More Storage Space

Files that are deleted are sent to the Trash. This means that even though you have deleted the file or folder, it will still take up storage space. To free up or reclaim your space, you'll have to go to the online Trash and delete those files.

This cannot be done from the sync client that you've installed on your computer. Login to Drive's web interface and from the left sidebar, click on the "More" link and then you'll see the Trash option.

Click on the "Empty trash" button to empty the trash and delete all files, or if you prefer to delete selected files then you can do that too.

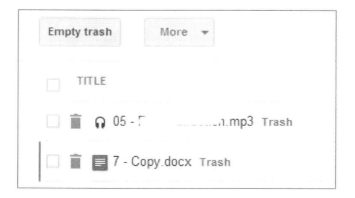

Do this and you'll free up storage space on your Drive account.

Automate Tasks in your Google Drive using IFTTT

IFTTT, known as If This Then That is a web app that has recently become very popular. IFTTT lets you automate and combine various tasks and events between different web services that you use. For example, you can configure IFTTT such that whenever you save a new photo with the help of Instagram, it will be automatically added to Drive. This is just one example and IFTTT can do much more than this.

We can combine IFTTT with Drive and create recipes. A recipe is a combination of trigger and an action.

If this seems interesting to you, then let's discuss about some recipes that works with Drive. Below you can find some ready-made recipes that you can start using right now. If you're new to IFTTT, then you'll first need to create an account and authorize IFTTT to use your Drive account.

1. Backup iOS (iPhone) contacts to a Google Spreadsheet. Recipe URL: https://ifttt.com/recipes/102384
2. Add files to Google Drive from Dropbox. Recipe URL https://ifttt.com/recipes/102384
3. Copy new Instagram picture directly to Google Drive. Recipe URL: https://ifttt.com/recipes/102384
4. Upload new iOS photos to Google Drive. Recipe URL: https://ifttt.com/recipes/102384
5. Track Foursquare check-ins (with Maps) in a Google Drive Spreadsheet. Recipe URL: https://ifttt.com/recipes/58835
6. Save all photos that are uploaded to Facebook on Google Drive. Recipe URL: https://ifttt.com/recipes/54781
7. Send tagged photos from Facebook to Google Drive. Recipe URL: https://ifttt.com/recipes/84532
8. Add read items to Google Drive as PDFs. Recipe URL: https://ifttt.com/recipes/54723
9. Add Feedly subscriptions to Google Spreadsheet. Recipe URL: https://ifttt.com/recipes/102138

10. Save Name+URL of favorite YouTube songs to a spreadsheet in Drive. Recipe URL: https://ifttt.com/recipes/58680

There are many more recipes that you can search on IFTTT that are related to Drive. In the IFTTT site, search for the term "Drive" and you'll get plethora of recipes related to it. You can either try out those ready-made recipes or create your own recipe.

Welcome to a faster, smarter and automated Drive.

About The Author

My name is Saqib Khan and I am a technology enthusiast. I've been helping people understand technical stuff from quite a long time. I've been blogging on technostarry.com from a long time, where I usually write how-to's on various tech topics.

I hope this book will help you to master Drive. What makes it special is that it not only offers file storage, syncing and collaboration, but it also offers a full-fledged online office suite which means you won't need to figure out how would you open or edit your office file. If you have an office file in your Drive, then you can do just about anything with it. Even if you don't plan on using the office features, you can use Drive to store and sync your files across different devices.

If you want to stay connected with me, then you can follow me on Twitter at http://twitter.com/technostarry. I can also be reached from saqib@technostarry.com. Should you have any questions, problems or suggestions regarding this book, you can connect with me on Twitter or Email and I will get back to you.

Also if you're stuck somewhere, then you can refer to Google Drive's official support page from https://support.google.com/drive/?hl=en.

If you've liked this book, then you might also want to check out my other books on Amazon by searching for "Saqib Khan" in the search field. I've also written books on Dropbox, Microsoft OneDrive, and 70 Must-Have and Essential Android apps which you can check out from Amazon.

Lastly, I would like to thank you for taking the time to read this book. I wish you all the best for the future.

Saqib Khan

Printed in Great Britain
by Amazon.co.uk, Ltd.,
Marston Gate.